FULL METAL CHALLENGE

FULL METAL CHALLENGE

METAL MANIA

The Full Inside Story of the Machines,
their Makers and the Mechanical Madness

Text by Marcus Hearn
Photographs by Fabio Calascibetta

TED SMART

To Richard,
who could show this lot a thing or two behind the wheel

This edition produced for The Book People Ltd, Hall Wood Avenue, Haydock, St Helens WA11 9UL

First published in Great Britain in 2003

10 9 8 7 6 5 4 3 2 1

Text and photographs © RDF Media, 2003

RDF Media Limited have asserted their right to be identified as the author of this work under the Copyright, Designs and Patents Act 1988.

www.rdfmedia.com

First published by
Ebury Press
Random House, 20 Vauxhall Bridge Road,
London SW1V 2SA

Random House Australia (Pty) Limited
20 Alfred Street, Milsons Point, Sydney,
New South Wales 2061, Australia

Random House New Zealand Limited
18 Poland Road, Glenfield, Auckland 10,
New Zealand

Random House South Africa (Pty) Limited
Endulini, 5A Jubilee Road, Parktown 2193,
South Africa

The Random House Group Limited Reg. No. 954009

www.randomhouse.co.uk

A CIP catalogue record for this book is available from the British Library.

Cover Design by PUSH
Text design and typesetting by PUSH

Papers used by Ebury Press are natural, recyclable products made from wood grown in sustainable forests.

Printed and bound by APPL Wemding, Germany.

RDF MEDIA

Contents

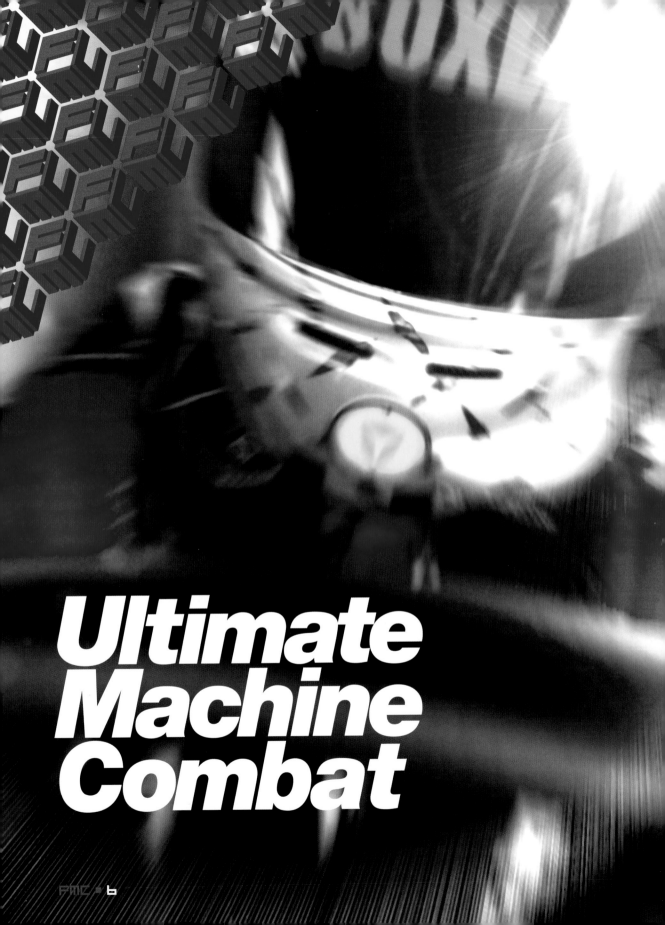

Ultimate Machine Combat

A disused power station on the southern coast of England is about to play host to an extraordinary contest. The gladiators in this dangerous sport have had just one month to create and test their weapons of choice – full-sized vehicles which they have designed, and which they will ride into battle.

Twenty-seven teams from twelve countries have converged on this site with their extraordinary machines, intent on out-running, out-manoeuvring or simply overpowering their opponents to grab the title Full Metal Challenge World Champion.

The teams will lock horns across nine bizarre games in a nightmarish fairground scenario that will test every aspect of their vehicles' capabilities. This is the Road Rage Olympics and there can be only one winner.

Machines that can take 30 days to build can take only 30 seconds to destroy…

It all started with a proposal for a new series called Death Race 2000, written by a crazed boy I work with called Dominic. He's the sort of person who would have a small but crucial role in a heist movie as the teenager who, while eating a huge unhealthy burger and complaining about the state of gherkins nowadays, hacks into the Pentagon's computer system.

Dom had been talking to me about how 'all those robot shows' were rubbish because they were just TOO SMALL and because there WEREN'T REAL WEAPONS and because things didn't BLOW UP ENOUGH. Although he is insane, he had a point. And it got us thinking about doing something that was – well – really really big.

We wanted teams from all over the world, sets that were like sets from movies, games that were spectacular and twisted, machines that made your hair stand on end. And, most importantly, we didn't want people on the end of a remote-controlled device; we wanted them behind the wheel.

Two years on and here is Full Metal Challenge. We ditched the weapons and a few other things along the way, but hope we kept the whole mutant fun house thing. It took about six months to find our 27 teams from five continents but it was worth every moment of the hunt – their machines took our breath away. It took almost as long to turn our location from a derelict power station into a kind of Disneyland of beautiful, sumptuous sets and games that wouldn't look out of place at Alton Towers. Well, if the nice people at Alton Towers didn't mind you going on their rides in your car.

And what else? Well Henry Rollins is clearly a previously undiscovered element. Probably called something like Rocknrollesium. An element with an atomic number of about a billion.

And that's it really. Hopefully it is something like there has never quite been before. Oh, except I was a huge It's a Knockout fan when I was a kid and I hope it shows.

Cathy Rogers
London
October 2002

In April of 2002, Cathy Rogers contacted me and asked if I want to meet and discuss possible involvement with a new show she was working on called Full Metal Challenge. I was given a brief rundown of the show and what my job would be. I said yes to the meeting.

I met up with her at a coffee place in Los Angeles. While explaining the show to me, she pulled out rough sketches of the games and said that the cars would be actual size and that it was all for real, etc. I tried to imagine the size of the games and the set and the whole thing and it was fairly impossible. It seemed too huge and ambitious to actually pull off. Cathy said that it was all in motion and would I be interested in doing some screen testing for the possibility of co-presenting the show with her? Of course I agreed.

We met days later on the set of Junkyard Wars (the US name for Scrapheap Challenge) and shot some segments for the folks at The Learning Channel and Channel 4 to see. It seemed to go well. I went back home hoping I could possibly be part of this very cool project.

Several days later I get a letter from Cathy telling me that I have the job if I want it. I couldn't believe my luck. I knew this was going to be great.

As much as I had tried to imagine what the set would look like, nothing prepared me for the awesome size and construction of Full Metal Challenge. Much bigger than I thought it would be. Huge. Insane. My kind of place.

The next five weeks were a hardworking, focused, adrenalised blur. All of a sudden I was on a plane back to LA. What a trip.

We have a show! The vehicles were great win or lose. The cooling towers where Sumo, Pitball and Bumper Cars took place will go on record as some of the best shooting locations ever. Rollercoaster is ultimate. Great driving, great competition. There's nothing like Full Metal Challenge anywhere. I am very proud of the small part I played in this epic. Bam!

Henry Rollins
Los Angeles
October 2002

The Beginnings

FMC ▪ 14

To discover the origins of *Full Metal Challenge*, we need to go back seven years to a grimy scrapheap in Bristol. *Scrapheap Challenge*, the factual entertainment show that made its debut on Channel 4 in 1996, was unlike anything British television had seen before. The programme is produced by RDF Media (the name is made up from the initials of founders Richard Dove and David Frank), the company which is also responsible for such successful programmes as *Banzai*, *Faking It* and *House Moves From Hell*.

The ingenious format makes for compelling viewing: two teams of enterprising mechanics are given just one day to build a contraption of the producers' choice, using parts they salvage from a scrapheap. They are given all the space and tools they need, but apart from that they're on their own. Over the last five series the numerous teams have successfully cobbled together such diverse creations as an amphibious vehicle, a diving bell and a medieval siege engine.

Scrapheap Challenge is co-presented by Robert Llewellyn, a comedian and actor previously best known for his portrayal of the endearing household robot Kryten in the BBC's sci-fi sitcom *Red Dwarf*. 'The underlying drive of *Scrapheap Challenge* is educational,' he says. 'Any complex engineering subject is looked at in detail with either a team-member or the challenge judge explaining it to me, and if I understand it, anyone can. Through the use of wonderfully clear graphics, any complex area of engineering is explored in detail, and then the concept can be seen being used in the machine.'

The autumn 2002 series of *Scrapheap Challenge* was hosted by Llewellyn and former *Big Breakfast* presenter Lisa Rogers, but Robert hosted the previous three series with Cathy Rogers (no relation). Cathy took a break from *Scrapheap* to begin preparing RDF's latest venture – a follow-up series with a similar engineering theme but a more ambitious scale.

Cathy graduated from Oxford in 1990 with a 'nice but useless' degree and went to medical school for a while before joining television production company Diverse. She joined RDF in 1995 to work on science documentaries, and soon became the company's Head of Science. She is now one of the company's directors and president of its Los Angeles branch. 'I became a presenter kind of by accident,' she explains bashfully. 'The first series of *Scrapheap Challenge* was presented by Robert,

and when that finished we took a look at the format and decided that there were a few biggish things that we wanted to change. For example, in the first series we had the same teams in every episode, and we followed them over the whole seven weeks, getting to know them. I though this was good, but not as good as having two rival teams building towards a final. So we changed that, and then decided it would be good to have another presenter to make things a bit easier for Robert. As it was, he was having to do the voice-overs for the graphics explaining all the engineering concepts, and then we'd show him pointing to something the team had built and asking them how that bit in the middle worked. The show really needed two people, two voices. We started looking around, and decided quite early on that the other presenter should be a woman because *Scrapheap* is such a male-dominated show. I auditioned quite a lot of people that I liked, but with presenters you have to put them all past Channel 4 and for whatever reasons they didn't like who we were coming up with. Channel 4 eventually suggested that I should be Robert's co-presenter because I was producing it anyway and they wanted someone who was scientifically inclined, which I am. At first I said, "Don't be ridiculous," but then I thought about it and said, "All right then, I'll give it a go."'

Cathy was wearing her producer's hat when she started thinking about a follow-up to *Scrapheap Challenge*. She was initially inspired by Dominic McCarthy, a colleague in Los Angeles who was a fan of the 1975 movie *Death Race 2000*, which starred David Carradine and Sylvester Stallone (tagline: 'In the year 2000 hit and run driving is no longer a felony – it's the national sport!').

'He was talking around that,' says Cathy, 'and I think it became one of those situations where the name made the idea. The show would have seen lots of teams building vehicles, and then we'd fly over them in helicopters, drop bombs on them and fire on them with cannons. In order to survive, the teams would have had to have gone underwater and things like that. It was exciting but it was a bit extreme – particularly in light of the 11 September attacks in America – but what stayed with me was the fact that there was nothing remotely polite about it as a format. It was the sheer audacity that got us thinking.

'The other inspiration, which was slightly more down to earth, came from a *Scrapheap Challenge* special where we extended the format further and had three teams instead of the usual two. One team was British, one was American and the other came from Russia. The game was bigger and was held over a few days. Having the Russian team there made it feel so much more exciting and important and worthwhile. Looking back at it I think that was the start of the new show – Dom's audacity and the Russians' charm.'

Cathy called the new programme *Full Metal Challenge* and devised a contest that takes place on a truly global scale. *Full Metal Challenge* features 27 teams from five continents – nine of the teams are from the United Kingdom; nine are from the United States and Canada and the remaining nine are from Australia, Chile, China, Iceland, Germany, India, New Zealand, Russia and South Africa. Potential contestants were told that they would be given £2000/$3000 and 30 days in which to build a vehicle to take part in the competition. Other than being obliged to comply with a set of strict safety guidelines, the contestants were given free reign when designing their vehicles and told next-to-nothing about the nature of the games they would be taking part in.

Before the search for contestants began, however, Cathy set to work devising the nine games that would comprise the *Full Metal Challenge* experience. She dreamed up the various tournaments in Los Angeles, working alongside Greg Bryant, the chief engineering consultant on *Junkyard Wars* and *Scrapheap Challenge*. Greg has gained considerable experience on a wide variety of unusual projects: he was the engineering manager for robotics system integration aboard the NASA space station, and also provided location technical support for James Cameron's pioneering underwater drama *The Abyss*. 'Working on *The Abyss* was the crossover point in my career from what I call mainstream engineering into the real abyss – entertainment engineering,' he says.

For eight years Greg worked as the technical director of show mechanical engineering at Walt Disney Imagineering, designing rides and animated shows. He was also project manager at Universal Studios, responsible for designing and building millions of dollars' worth of shows and rides at the Orlando theme park, including Ghostbusters and the new Jaws ride. For *Full Metal Challenge*, he and Cathy came up with a surreal fairground-style course comprising giant versions of such popular games as ten pin

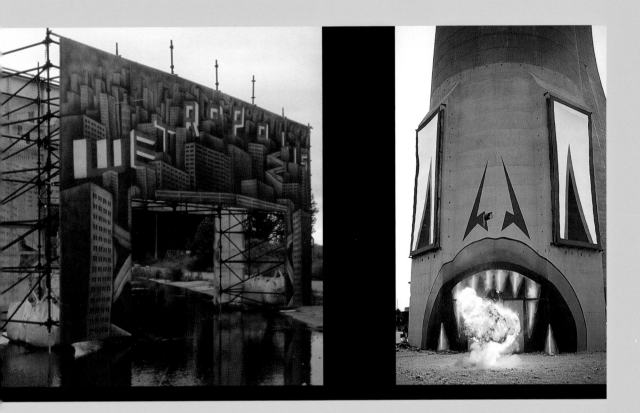

bowling and bumper cars. Greg explains that safety was always foremost in his mind: 'The rules specified that the vehicles would be involved in collisions and needed to be designed and built accordingly. Each vehicle's weight was not to exceed 3000 kilograms. Also, because there is no limit to people's creativity in some areas, we specified that the vehicles could only be built with defensive and not offensive capabilities. The rules also went into roll cage design in great detail because of our expectation that not all the vehicles would get through certain events without going over on their side. Our basic assumption was that drivers dressed in good safety equipment inside a safely constructed vehicle with a well designed and built roll cage which could withstand reasonable collisions and rollovers safely. Our engineers inspected the vehicles during the build to make sure they would be both durable and safe.

'The rules also described important performance capabilities that each vehicle should have,' he continues. 'We designed the games in such a way that all the vehicles entering would be able to compete effectively, regardless of their type. Each game tests the vehicles in different ways. In order to reduce the severity of vehicle impacts the events were designed to limit either the length that vehicles could accelerate, to have slick surfaces to reduce traction, or to have obstacles placed which kept vehicle speeds relatively low. Each game also has water-filled traffic barriers either surrounding the event or placed in locations to protect both the drivers and the crew around the event.'

'The games came first,' adds Cathy, 'but the location did have an important influence. I worked on the games with Greg in LA, but I kept coming back to England to visit the people who were recruiting the teams and to look at potential sites. When we found the site that we chose I knew straight away that we had to have it. We were about three-quarters of the way through working out the games when we found the site, and we immediately started adapting the games to the new possibilities it offered us.'

The site Cathy and the team chose was the vast Richborough Power Station in Sandwich, Kent. The power station was opened in 1963, and was originally a coal-burning facility. It was converted to the controversial Orimulsion burning process before its last owners, Powergen, closed it down in September 1997. Powergen still operates a 1 MW wind turbine on the Minster Marshes, just beyond

the station's three cavernous cooling towers, but the site itself had been reduced to the level of a near-derelict shell by the time RDF leased it from its present owners.

The most striking thing about Richborough is its size. The site is approximately one-and-a-quarter miles from end-to-end, and a tour of its hollow, echoing buildings is an eerie experience. Crumbling concrete is fast giving way to the weeds that grow through the cracks in the ground, and potholes litter the pathways that connect the various buildings. About a month after work began converting the site, the *FMC* production team brought golf buggies in which to get around. During pre-production and production the battered vehicles were relied upon to get between the production office and some of the furthest flung games such as Wetropolis and Rollercoaster. The buggies are surprisingly nippy, but the gaping potholes and rubble-strewn fissures often make their journeys highly precarious.

'This was a model power station when it was built,' says RDF's site manager Alex Mahoney. 'It was obviously in a state of disrepair when we came here, but you can tell just by walking around some of the out buildings and office blocks that this was a prestigious installation – the types of doors and flooring that were used were of a very high quality. They even planted roses bushes around the entrance, so they must have had their own gardener!'

The mechanical contractor Chris French, of Steel Monkey, and the site general contractor Roger Chopping, of Project 42, headed the teams that transformed the site from a disused power station to the surreal *FMC* set in just eight weeks over summer 2002. 'I arrived here on 16 May,' says Alex, 'and it was about a week to ten days after that that we started preparing the workshop for the teams' vehicles and the production office. For the production office we had to convert the old sports and social club – we had to rip out all the seating and the stage.

'I've done outdoor stuff before but nothing like this,' he continues. 'This is huge, and by its very nature this is a dangerous place. Part of what we did in the early weeks was to make the site safe for everyone who arrived there afterwards to install the show equipment. The cooling towers were submerged in about four feet of water which had to be pumped out over and over again before the floors of the games could be installed. One thing we've always battled against on this site is the weather – when it changes it changes very fast and very dramatically. It's quite exposed and on some days it's a dust bowl with little dust devils spinning round the site and getting in your eyes. On other days you can be up against 65mph gusts and electrical storms. The first day I came here I was with Greg Bryant and Roger Chopping. I remember we were standing just off-centre inside one of the towers. We were leaning into the wind, and we were only two or three feet away from each other, but the wind was so strong that we had to scream just to make ourselves heard.'

Visitors to the site are rarely able to resist the opportunity to walk inside one of the cooling towers, onto the floor of one the games they contain – Pitball, Bumper Cars or Sumo – and gaze up through the top of the tower at the distant circle of sky that lies beyond. Intricate lighting rigs suspend row upon row of powerful lamps that are trained on the outlandish and colourful arenas below.

'The guys who were putting the lighting rigs inside the towers were on cherry pickers that went up 185 feet,' says Alex. 'That took them about halfway up the towers so they could drill points for the plates that held the rigs in place. It got especially difficult for them when it was raining. The rain would fall down into the tower, but the wind would come through the legs at the base and blow it back upwards. The rain would swirl around in the middle of the tower – about where these guys were in their baskets – and get mixed up with brick dust. The result was a mess of a whirlwind that made it very difficult to see anything.'

A fourth, much smaller, tower has been given a garish paint job and turned into 'The Chimney of Death' – teams that are knocked out of the competition are forced to watch as their vehicles are driven into the incinerator. Once they are consumed by the flames inside they appear to explode.

While development began on the site in Kent, Cathy and Greg worked on the games in Los Angeles and the London office of RDF continued recruiting contestants from all over the world. Some teams were invited to apply because they had been particularly noteworthy contestants on *Scrapheap Challenge* (or were promising teams who were just too late to be accepted for the latest series) but the majority were recruited from those that responded to advertisements that appeared on numerous websites around the world.

Each application had to be accompanied by a short video, in which the prospective team had to illustrate a mechanical or engineering principle in a concise and entertaining way. Thirty teams were selected (including one reserve team from each of the British, North American and international categories) and 27 of those were allocated places in the first nine shows – three teams in each heat. Episodes 10 to 12 will feature the nine semi-finalists, while the grand final will see the best three teams competing to win the *Full Metal Challenge* trophy and the considerable honour of being the programme's first world champions.

Cathy admits that she is disappointed that only four of the 81 contestants are female (all three members of The Flamin' Aussies and one member of The Bodysnatchers) but says that RDF made a real effort to encourage applications from women. 'After every series of *Scrapheap Challenge* we think we've cracked it and that we're going to receive lots of applications from women but it hasn't quite happened yet,' she laments. 'The shows are good, but I think they would be better if there was more of a mix. I know girls watch the shows, and I hope they will watch *Full Metal Challenge*. I've had letters from girls who love *Scrapheap* – they're aged between eight and 15 and they love doing science at school and they like making things. I think there is a stereotypical view that girls are good at crafts and techy stuff is for boys. One of the things I have always liked about *Scrapheap Challenge* is that it shows people making animate devices out of inanimate objects. I think that taps into a passion that some people have, irrespective of their gender. Unfortunately I think women are put off by the fact that the programmes seem so male-orientated. I also think that at the stage we're at now women probably feel as though they would have to offer an explanation as to why they're there. I'm really glad the Australian team is here, but I think they expected to be treated in a certain way, simply because they're women. We've got engineers who are here to help everyone out if they need it; they're just as prepared to help the Australian team as they are the Chinese team. I understand the Australians have been a bit prickly, maybe feeling that they've been offered help because they're women.'

In keeping with the international feel of the new programme, *Full Metal Challenge* is a co-production with The Learning Channel in the United

States. TLC has already enjoyed considerable success screening *Scrapheap Challenge* under the title *Junkyard Wars* and was happy to join forces with RDF for the new venture. The added financial clout enabled the shift in location from the relatively modest confines of *Scrapheap Challenge* to the sprawling location for the new programme. It was understood from the outset that *Full Metal Challenge* would have two presenters – one British and one American. The American's shoes were filled by cultural provocateur and Grammy Award-winner Henry Rollins. Between 1980 and 1986 man-mountain Rollins was the lead singer of Black Flag, one of America's most admired and controversial punk groups. He went on to front the successful Rollins Band, and is now an accomplished poet, spoken-word artist, publisher, stand-up comedian and actor, with appearances in *Johnny Mnemonic*, *Heat* and *Lost Highway*.

'The truth is, I wanted someone I thought would look good in a disused power station,' says Cathy. 'That is, someone with a presence big enough that he wouldn't be overshadowed by 300-foot high cooling towers.'

Henry is certainly difficult to ignore. On the rare moments he keeps still – such as when he intensely follows the progress of one of the vehicles around a course – he gives the impression of having been carved from granite. The contrast with the willowy Cathy couldn't be greater. When the camera is on him, Rollins seems to explode with genuine exuberance and is clearly fired up by the whole outlandish scenario. A talented wordsmith, Rollins' physical exuberance is matched by his colourful evocations of the tense atmosphere prior to the games and the adrenalin-rush of the contests. Between takes, he prowls the various courses like a cross between a caged animal and a curious child, inspecting their various facets with seemingly intense fascination. 'Cathy does the interviews and I am the colour man,' he says in gravelly tones. 'It's been one big summer of improv, which is what I like.

'There is often a correlation between the contestants and their vehicles,' he continues. 'The macho guys have macho vehicles, but it's not always the biggest one that wins. A fast car or a big battering-ram-type vehicle might help in one or two events but make you lose in another. Adaptability is the key.'

Cathy has resigned herself to another stint in front of the camera. 'I think of myself as a producer,' she asserts. 'I still don't think of presenting as a proper job. I do enjoy presenting but I find it

quite stressful. Generally speaking I'm not fond of presenters as a breed; I can't help thinking that they're acting and they usually are. Like newscasters, they speak in a strange way, pronouncing sentences in a way that no-one else would ever consider. I try to be completely normal when I'm presenting – I really try not to act, but it's very difficult when you're surrounded by cameras and you have to do things over and over again. If I had to choose between presenting and producing I would definitely choose producing. I certainly don't think I could present something that wasn't mine. I just wouldn't be able to do it.'

Filming began on *Full Metal Challenge* in July 2002, and the team were relieved that the weather seemed to dramatically improve. 'It was often quite hot and sunny,' says Greg. 'Further evidence that Cathy Rogers really is a goddess!'

Filming is overseen by director Julia Knowles, who co-ordinates the multitude of swooping and zooming cameras from inside a truck stationed on the site. Julia specialises in directing live events for television, and has previously tackled such mindboggling spectacles as the *MTV Europe Music Awards* and the BBC's *Millennium Celebration* from the London Dome (featuring a full orchestra, a 200-strong choir, aero ballet and a promenade carnival).

'There have been a few headaches but I'm very glad that we're able to do *Full Metal Challenge* from such an unusual location,' says Alex Mahoney. 'I don't think we'd have achieved the same effect if we'd have shot this in a studio. Take the Sumo game for example, which is one of the ones that is

shot inside one of the cooling towers. We wait until it's dark when we shoot that, and the lights suspended in the tower augment whatever light is outside. It looks fantastic, and it's a unique effect. The cooling towers are monoliths that you just couldn't recreate in a studio, and if the weather changes then I hope we'll find a way to incorporate that into the programme so it actually enhances the mood.'

'Sumo is my favourite game,' says Henry. 'It has a Three Mile Island-look, with great lighting. Engines are screaming in vehicular pain and the smoke and noise are unbelievable.'

Cathy is optimistic that there will be a second series of *Full Metal Challenge*, but she has yet to sufficiently recover from the rigours of series one to consider what it might contain. '*Full Metal Challenge* is so big that at the moment what I feel like doing the most is something that's the extreme opposite,' she says, laughing. 'I'd quite like to do an archaic documentary about bacteria that live on moss! But seriously, in an ideal world I think I'd like to do a series of *Full Metal Challenge* in a different country each year, a bit like the Olympics or the World Cup, but I suspect that's just not practical. If we do another series I think it will be on a different site, but one that hopefully has just as strong an identity as the one we're using now.'

In conclusion, I ask Cathy what car she drives herself, and whether she has a dream vehicle. Her response is possibly the biggest revelation so far. 'It's confession time,' she exclaims, throwing her hands up in the air. 'I'm afraid I haven't even got a car – I ride a bicycle!'

The UK Teams and Vehicles

The Aquaholics/Octopush
The Battle Bodgers/Pure Adrenalin
The Bodysnatchers/Stomp
The Dodgy Oppos/The Wolverine
The Have A Go Likelies/The Devil's Mule
The Mud Hatters/Mega Hurtz
The Pole Cats/White Noise
The Tartan Tinkerers/Spartacus
Three Shades of Grey/Wild Thing

North American Teams and Vehicles

The Ball and Chain Gang/Idiodyssey
Chicago Fire/911
The Country Boys/The Southern Crusher
The Death Guild/Monkey
The Hot Rods/The Double Dubb
The Law Dawgs/Impact Weapon
The Snowdiggers/Steel Survivor (Canada)
Tribal Force/Rez Ride
The Washburns/The Agrivator

International Teams and Vehicles

The Autobahn Boys/Humungus (Germany)
The Desert Pumas/Marabunta (Chile)
The Flamin' Aussies/The Deflector (Australia)
Flying Horse/The Flying Horse (China)
The Ice Vikings/Thor (Iceland)
Indian Hope Trick/Delhi Belly (India)
The Kalahari Cats/The Leopard (South Africa)
Kiwi Thunder/Black Thunder (New Zealand)
The Russian Bears/The Siberian Monster (Russia)

The Aquaholics
Dorset, United Kingdom

Adam Kyte (aka Pike)
Team captain Pike loves sailing, competes in 4x4 trials and flies light aircraft and micro-lights. He has a cheerful philosophy: 'Don't miss an opportunity – it might come disguised as hard work.'

Martyn Pitman
At just 21 years of age, Martyn is one of the youngest competitors in *Full Metal Challenge*. He describes Pike and Tony as 'the brains', but his team-mates know he is multi-skilled. Martyn loves tinkering with cars, and has spent about £7,000 renovating a 33-year-old Mark 1 Mini pick-up. He estimates that the vehicle is now worth... about £7,000.

Tony Stankus
Tony is the senior member of the team, and has significant experience with powerboats and hovercraft. He boasts that he 'can breathe life into anything!' A keen off-roader, he dreams of one day competing in the Paris-Dakar Rally with his wife.

Adam, Martin and Tony are all engineers for the Royal National Lifeboat Institute (RNLI) so it is only fitting that their *Full Metal Challenge* vehicle was designed on a boat. The team convened aboard the yacht owned by captain Adam 'Pike' Kyte and – after an intense evening's work – came up with one of the most distinctive vehicles in the entire competition.

'We knew it was going to be difficult getting into the competition because RDF had already warned us that there were hundreds of entrants for the nine British places available,' says Tony. 'So we knew we had to come up with a special design.'

The team felt compelled to devise something that was in some way related to water. They had got as far as devising a vehicle called The Lobster – so-named because of its pincer-like arms – when Pike's girlfriend Kelly suggested they instead design a car based on an octopus. 'It was one of those inspirational things,' says Tony, who immediately set to work with Pike on a new design.

'Tony and I worked on the concept,' says Pike, 'and I did all the work on the computer. When we started building it, Martyn had a lot of input, suggesting simpler alternatives and so on. I'm glad it was a team effort, because if only one of us had sat down and done the design I don't think it would have come out as well. Everybody had different ideas, and in the end a compromise was the best solution. I think we all contributed an equal number of ideas in the end.'

The result is Octopush, a bizarre vehicle with two engines, eight wheels and tentacle-like bars that the team hope will serve as protection from side-impact.

'The tentacles were originally going to be more elaborate,' says Tony, 'but towards the end of the build time we had temporal failure – we ran out of time! It was just impossible to get it all together. If I've got any advice for other people wanting to try this it would be: Don't try to be as mechanically inventive as we have, because you'll just be making yourself a huge pile of work.'

Teething Trouble

During testing, Pike took the Octopush up a steep ridge. When the vehicle came down the other side it nose-dived into a deep rut. 'We got the vehicle out, but found that the tow bar had been bent,' says Martyn. 'We were able to take it off, straighten it and put it back on again, but then we found that the steering was misaligned. We couldn't work out what it was, until someone pointed out that the steering lock had moved – we'd jumped a couple of teeth. We did some analysis and fixed it, but I'm of the opinion that it wasn't adjusted properly at the start. I don't think it would have been able to jump like that unless it had been bent.'

Octopush

DONOR VEHICLE
Two 3.5 V8 Range Rovers

ENGINE TYPE
Two 3.5L EFI V8 Range Rover
150 bhp each

TRANSMISSION TYPE
Range auto boxes

ESTIMATED WEIGHT
2.99 tons

OVERALL LENGTH
14.6 feet

SUSPENSION TYPE
Modified Range Rover –
radius arms, coil springs etc

FUEL TYPE
Petrol

OTHER FEATURES
Eight-wheel drive, four-wheel steer

The Autobahn Boys
Bremen, Germany

Udo Fink

Team captain Heinz Udo Fink owns his own auto workshop. He has worked with numerous racing teams as an engineer and counts drag racing and demolition derbies among his hobbies. His chief passion, however, is restoring classic cars. 'I'm really a car guy,' he says. 'I spend my time playing with my son with cars, or with my son's cars, or with my cars... that's it really.'

Ulrich Weinberg (aka Uli)

Uli owns a bodywork repair shop and has hand-built over 40 cars entirely from parts he has made himself. 'One should make everything by hand,' he claims, and proves it by building cars that don't exist any more, working purely from photographs.

Christian Diakmann

Main driver Christian only became interested in cars when he left the German Air Force following a parachuting accident when he was 25. Now 34, Christian loves anything to do with engines and has designed and built ten motorbikes. Christian works with Uli at his shop during the day, and at weekends indulges one of his other great passions - rockabilly music.

The German team's first impression of England was formed on the journey from Gatwick Airport. Gazing out of the windows of their car they registered mild surprise at the relatively slow speed of the British motorway traffic. 'We're all about speed,' explains Udo Fink in matter-of-fact way. 'That's why we're called The Autobahn Boys.'

There was more disappointment just around the corner when the team discovered that UK licensing laws were rather different from what they were used to. In Germany, some pubs close as late as 6.00 am, and a few stay open for 24 hours. England's draconian licensing laws turned out to be a blessing in disguise, however, as the *Full Metal Challenge* schedule demanded some early morning starts for the contestants.

The Autobahn Boys are a grizzled bunch who look as though they've just crawled from a nearby trench. Scratch the crusty surface of their battle-weary demeanour and a cool pragmatism is soon revealed.

'We decided from the start to keep our design as simple as possible,' says Uli, describing their vehicle, Humungus. 'Three thousand Euros is not very much money, so we knew we wouldn't be able to afford any expensive components. If you were to compare Humungus to a dog, I think it would a shepherd dog, as opposed to a pit bull or a bloodhound. In other words, I think we've made a good all-rounder. There are no gimmicks on our machine, but I think it can do anything.'

The most expensive elements of Humungus were the engine (the donor vehicle was a 450hp Chevy) and the tyres. If the vehicle is successful, it will be at least partly due to a cool mix of ingenuity and solid engineering. The driver, Christian, is seated mid-chassis, giving him good all-round vision. Humungus's impressive horsepower is matched by superb suspension - any wheel can lift over two feet off the ground before any of the other wheels is destabilised. The locked central differential means that the vehicle has good traction, even on slippery surfaces.

'No mercy no limits!'

'There are no gimmicks on our machine, but I think it can do anything'

'We know that water will be involved somewhere,' says Uli, considering the nature of the various courses, ' but other than that we don't know if we're going to be driving on mud, gravel, asphalt or whatever, but we're confident - we have a strong, four-wheel drive vehicle. We'll be formidable out there - no mercy, no limits!'

The team constructed Humungus in Uli's garage, struggling to find the time to realise what, by their own admission, was a fairly simple design. 'I think 30 days would have been enough time for a team that didn't have regular jobs,' says Christian, 'but we each had our own work to attend to and families waiting for us so that made it especially difficult, especially at the weekends. During the week we had to find the time and energy to work on Humungus after we had spent eight hours working on other cars.'

'Business always came first,' nods Uli. 'For us this competition is a hobby - if you spend too much time on your hobby it becomes a problem anyway.' As the deadline drew closer, such finishing touches as the more elaborate paint-job the team originally intended were abandoned. The little time left at the end of the schedule was used to take Humungus on a high-speed test-drive across a field where the brakes, suspension and engine transmission were all evaluated. When the team was reunited with the vehicle in England, just before filming began, they tested the vehicle one more time on heavy terrain.

'We were surprised,' says Christian, 'because the vehicle performed much better than we originally expected.'

'Its strongest aspect is its acceleration,' says Uli. 'And compared to some of the other vehicles we've seen in the workshop, I think ours is more compact and probably more manoeuvrable.'

'I think we were right to keep Humungus simple,' says Udo, summing up the team's experience so far. Christian agrees: 'We don't know what to expect out there - we have never seen *Scrapheap Challenge*, and I'm sure this is going to be different anyway - but I've learned that the two most important factors when you're preparing for the competition are testing and driving experience. You need the experience to know what needs changing when you are testing, and you need to keep the vehicle simple so you can change things quickly and easily.'

'We haven't tried to build the ultimate machine,' says Uli, 'but we know we have to come first in at least one of the courses in our heat. I don't think it's necessary to come first in every game in order to qualify for the next round. We aim to survive, partly because we know that the car that is always in front must be working very hard indeed, and we obviously don't want to risk breaking down.'

Whether this pragmatism will extend to Christian's driving technique remains to be seen. 'We're confident,' says Udo as the team trudge back to the workshop for more testing. 'Yeah,' adds Christian, 'we're cool as ice.'

Humungus

DONOR VEHICLE
Chevy Blazer K5

ENGINE TYPE
Chevy 45L 350bhp

TRANSMISSION TYPE
Automatic

ESTIMATED WEIGHT
1500 kg

OVERALL LENGTH
15 feet

WIDTH
7 feet 4 inches

HEIGHT
7 feet 4 inches

SUSPENSION TYPE
Leaf spring front, coil spring rear

FUEL TYPE
Petrol

OTHER FEATURES
Four-wheel drive

The Ball and Chain Gang
Washington State, USA

Tim Wiggans
Team captain Tim had a lot of experience to draw upon when he designed his team's vehicle: he spent eight years as a mechanic and four years as an army ranger. One of his more unusual hobbies is breeding Madagascar Hissing Cockroaches. 'They're usually jungle-dwellers,' says Tim, 'not the sort of insects you'd find under your refrigerator!'

James Collins
James is an electrical contractor but took time off to help construct the vehicle for *Full Metal Challenge*. In 1990 he joined Tim as a stock car driver, and now pursues other such diverse hobbies as off-roading and golf.

Robert Cochran
Before he became a painting contractor Robert worked as a commercial driver and spent time building aeroplane hangars at an air force base in Alaska. His hobbies include martial arts, and he possesses a second degree black belt in karate.

The Ball and Chain Gang share perhaps the most unusual bond of any team in *Full Metal Challenge* – Tim, James and Robert are all married to sisters from the same family. 'They were pretty supportive when we told them we wanted to enter the competition,' says James, the team's softly-spoken, tobacco-chewing co-driver. 'We told them about the schedule so they knew what to expect and they all said it was OK. All three are the type that don't go back on their word once they agree to something, and it worked out very well. It was tough when we were building the car – at one point I didn't see my family for a few days – but they were interested and supportive. And they were certainly glad to have us back at the end of the four weeks.'

'Because we all married into the same family we've known each other for quite some time,' says team captain Tim, a metal fabricator and blacksmith by trade. 'I've known Rob for 14 or 15 years and I've known James even longer. But when you work together as closely as we did for 30 days you sure get to know more about somebody. Speaking for myself, I'm glad to say that we were really honest with each other and it was a happy experience.'

The naming of the team's vehicle – the Idiodyssey – turned out to be a family affair as well. 'Idiodyssey is a term my wife and I came up with,' says Robert, laughing. 'It's a word we use to describe a journey that ends up being sidetracked – those odd things in life that happen to you whether they're your fault or not. You end up being an idiot on an odyssey – an idiodyssey!'

The Idiodyssey is a rugged four-wheel drive monster with steel armour-plating and chain-driven axles which offer higher-than-usual ground clearance. The vehicle started life in Tim's workshop as a combination of a truck and a race car, both donated by Robert. The body of the truck gave way to the lighter frame from the car, and although this combination of second-hand parts saved the team money it caused major headaches

'We wanted to deliver what we'd promised'

'The axle drops at the ends and is chain-driven down to the wheels'

for Tim and Robert, who did the welding. Once the initial work was completed, the roll cage, defensive caging, wheels and tyres all had to be paid for out of the team's $3000 budget.

Despite underestimating the cost of fusing the two machines, the team would have stayed on budget were it not for an expensive miscalculation. 'The axle drops at the ends and is chain-driven down to the wheels,' explains Robert. 'I designed the system, but I didn't have the technical data that I needed on machines, chains and sprockets to make this thing go. So that's where I relied on the skills of the chain manufacturer and took their advice on the size and shape of chain to use. So we assembled everything but we didn't have time to test it until quite late. We had probably only rolled it about six or eight feet when all the chains and sprockets exploded. They were very expensive to replace.'

Once new chains of a different specification had been purchased, there was a rush to make them fit. The team are now satisfied that their system works, and will give them an important edge in the competition. 'We can go over just about anything without catching it,' says James, 'so it really keeps our roll-centre low. We have really heavy tyres but they're not attached to the frame or body so the vehicle's light.'

These claims are no idle boast: during the last day of testing at the site, the Idiodyssey actually took to the air on four separate occasions - and each time all four wheels cleared the ground.

With construction time fast running out, the team were concerned that they wouldn't be able to fit the other unusual element of their vehicle. 'We've got two cockpits,' says Tim proudly, 'one facing to the front and one to the rear.' The disintegration of the original chain was a significant setback to the team, and towards the end they worked 36-40 hour stretches without a break in order to add the extra cockpit. 'I refused to abandon the idea,' says Tim. 'It was one of the designs that RDF had been most excited about and I wasn't prepared to let it go.' All three nod in agreement, with James adding: 'We wanted to deliver what we'd promised.'

Like all the teams, The Ball and Chain Gang received no specific information about any of the courses while they were designing and constructing their vehicle, so what prompted this eccentric addition?

'Anyone who has ever parallel parked will know how difficult it is,' says Tim. 'If you were sitting in the trunk with a steering wheel you'd find it a lot easier. It seems like the most natural thing in the world once you've actually done it - you can drive a car backwards and manoeuvre it much better going into reverse than you can sitting in the front looking over your shoulder. You wouldn't believe it, but we've built it and I've driven it - it works. The manoeuvrability increases by 90 per cent.'

The Ball and Chain Gang are big men with a bold ambition and a big vehicle. 'We're gonna win,' says James, 'because of our aggressive nature and never-say-die attitude. Lord knows we've proved that.'

'You wouldn't believe it,
but we've built it and I've
driven it — it works'

'We're gonna win!'

Idiodyssey

DONOR VEHICLE
GMC pick-up truck
Ford Pinto

ENGINE TYPE
350 Chev V8
175 bhp

TRANSMISSION TYPE
Chev 350 turbo

ESTIMATED WEIGHT
2400 kilograms

OVERALL LENGTH
16 feet

WIDTH
7 feet 6 inches

HEIGHT
7 feet 4 inches

SUSPENSION TYPE
Leaf spring

FUEL TYPE
Petrol

OTHER FEATURES
Four-wheel drive

Pre-flight Check

'Whatever concerns I may have had about the vehicle were erased when we finally got to test it,' said co-driver James immediately prior to filming The Ball and Chain Gang's first heat. 'I was very impressed with the stability and landing, and if I am pinched for time and find myself airborne I now know that I can land and keep on going, so I'll be able to catch up.' Fellow driver Robert expressed concerns about colliding with some of the opposing teams' vehicles, but was confident that the Idiodyssey would overcome whatever the courses had to offer. I can't wait to play the game and see what happens,' he said. 'Some people like to collect things – I like to collect experiences. This is going to be a great experience.'

Diary Extracts

Day 1
Today we rolled the car up on the truck frame and cut away the unwanted parts. The film crew seemed to get a kick out of it.

Day 5
11.oo pm – 1.oo am. It's very late. After 14 hours of alignment and fitting and realignment and welding the rear axle is assembled.

Day 7
After disassembling the front hubs I discovered that the axle U joints are bad and need to be replaced. It cost us another $50 at the parts store and another two hours of time. I do not need this now.

Day 19
We tested the axles today. The good news is it moves. The bad news is we keep breaking the chains. After checking the alignment of the sprockets and the tension on the chains I have come to the conclusion that the chains we were

advised to use are far too light for our application. (Cost of new chains: $500.)

Day 23
We all tackled the exoskeleton. It went perfectly. This thing is starting to look awesome.

Day 24
Rob and Jim fitted the seats and belts. Since the car has two cockpits all the controls are doubled up, so Jim is back to wiring switches.

Day 28
It took all night to remove the old chains and sprockets, and when I installed the new ones I found they were too long.

Day 29
My third day without sleep.

Day 30
Good night – I'm going to bed.

Ten Pin
Aim of the game: knock down the maximum number of skittles

This game kicks off each heat, and is one of the most spectacular and fast-moving events in Full Metal Challenge.

Ten Pin takes place in a huge bowling alley that has been constructed inside the biggest building on the site. One of the walls at either side of the alley has been removed, and most of the roof has also been taken away to facilitate a great view of the mayhem beneath for the watching cameras. The game begins when the car emerges from a special entrance at the back of the alley – the faces that decorate this garish portal belong to members of the FMC production team.

The vehicle has to run up to the bowling line to gain speed and momentum and head straight for the 12-foot high skittles arranged at the other end of the building. Each skittle weighs 150 pounds. The 30-metre bowling lane has a specially designed slippery surface which will make it difficult for all but the most skilful drivers to maintain an accurate course towards their goals. Just like ten pin bowling, each vehicle has two attempts at the skittles. The more skittles each vehicle knocks down, the more points there are for that team.

This is a unique and exacting test of each vehicle's speed and manoeuvrability.

43 ∎ FMG

The Rules

No stopping on the course is allowed until the vehicle has gone past the back row of the skittle formation. No reversing on the course is allowed. If a vehicle crosses the foul line, which is on the outside of the gutter (ie a vehicle would have to drive right over the gutter to the other side) that run will be null and void. The score is the total number of pins knocked down after two runs. The total maximum score is 20, which can only be achieved with two consecutive strikes.

45

The Battle Bodgers
Staffordshire, United Kingdom

Steve Atkin (aka Acker)
Team captain Acker was in the building trade before he started teaching design and technology. His experience with hydraulics and pneumatics came in handy when devising his team's front bumper, which can be used to ram or shove things that get in the way.

Phil Hopwood (aka Hoppy)
Hoppy is a sheet metal worker with excellent welding and fabricating skills. 'Our vehicle will be quick, agile and awesome,' he predicts, and is relishing the prospect of beating the German team.

Martin Mitchell (aka Magic)
Magic is an assistant factory manager, and the quietest member of an admittedly noisy team. Magic is also looking forward to beating the Germans, but reckons he can show the Americans a thing or two as well.

Horned, Viking-style helmets and other bygone implements of war are rested at the feet of The Battle Bodgers as they take a break from last-minute amendments to their vehicle. These raucous North Midlanders clearly mean business – but not necessarily under the bonnet of a car.

'We don't lack confidence when it comes to car mechanics,' admits team driver Magic, 'but we're not really into things like that compared to the other teams here. We tinker with the car on a Sunday, like most people, but we're not experts. We got to know each other through battle re-enactments, and we've been mates now for about 13 years.'

The Battle Bodgers have lived up to their name at a number of English Civil War battles re-enacted by the famous Sealed Knot Society. 'I think the greatest was the Battle of Ashby,' reminisces team captain Acker, 'even though we got our arses kicked! There must have been about 2000 people there.'

The Battle Bodgers' vehicle is called Pure Adrenalin (Hoppy: 'That's what it's going to be to watch it and that's what it's going to take to drive it!') and was largely designed by Magic, although the finished car was a joint effort. Of all the vehicles in the competition, Pure Adrenalin has the dubious distinction of being the one completed in the shortest time – a mere two weeks. 'We didn't have any choice,' says Acker, 'because I already had a two-week holiday booked. I spoke to the wife about postponing the holiday but she said "No way – the family has to come first." So we had to get it done it two weeks.'

Luckily, they had some help. 'Acker and me spent some time looking for a vehicle,' says Hoppy, 'and then we put something out on the internet, explaining what we were going to do and what we needed. At nine o'clock the next morning someone called Neil Bassett rang up and said, "No problem mate – I own a company that can help. I can supply the parts you need and you can use my place." We were very lucky to have met Neil.'

'It's got a lot of power in it – too much power, really'

'Neil showed us some vehicles,' recalls Magic, 'and offered one of them to us. We couldn't believe it because this thing was worth about £4000. And then he offered us the use of his premises. He's become the fourth member of our team, really.'

'All his advice was valuable to us,' continues Hoppy. 'If we were stuck we could ask Neil, "How does this work?" and he'd tell us without ever interfering with what we were doing. During the second week he went into hospital to have a brain tumour removed, but before he went he gave us the keys to the workshop and said, "Help yourself lads." He's been great.'

The punishing schedule meant that The Battle Bodgers only had one hour to test their vehicle, and that took place while a camera crew was there to record their progress. 'Prior to that we had driven it backwards and forwards in the workshop, but that was it,' says Acker. 'The first time it came out of the workshop we drove it round the car park for a while. We had a lot of problems: the battery didn't charge and the radiator overheated. We've solved those problems now, and when we tested it here we were the only team in our heat that didn't have difficulties. So, touch wood, I hope we'll be all right.'

Before the team arrived at the site they were uncomfortable about the fact that the front end of Pure Adrenalin was a bit light, making it unbalanced. They used their last-minute tinkering time to fill the box section of the front bumper with sand, ensuring that the front end now stays where it's supposed to when the vehicle is accelerating.

Magic is the first to refute Acker's suggestion that he asked for brown overalls before getting into the cockpit, but he concedes that he was 'a bit nervous' before he drove Pure Adrenalin for the first time. One would expect the combination of a 5.9 litre engine (the biggest single engine among the UK vehicles) and an unusual mid-chassis pivot to make the vehicle difficult to control. 'Actually it's easier than it looks,' says Magic. 'It reacts well to the steering and the back end shifts across so you can do the twist in it! It can be temperamental, and it hasn't got any suspension, except for the bit in the middle, but I'll be able to handle it.'

'I'm not comfortable in it,' admits Hoppy. 'When I had a go I realised how much power there was in it when I touched the accelerator. It's got a lot of power in it – too much power, really.'

The day before filming began, the team were buzzing with excitement even though they hadn't slept much the night before. 'We just weren't tired,' says Hoppy. 'We sat in Magic's room, going over everything, wondering if we should have done this or done that. Tomorrow morning it will all be up to Magic.'

'Hmmm,' frowns Magic. 'No sleep tonight either, I think.'

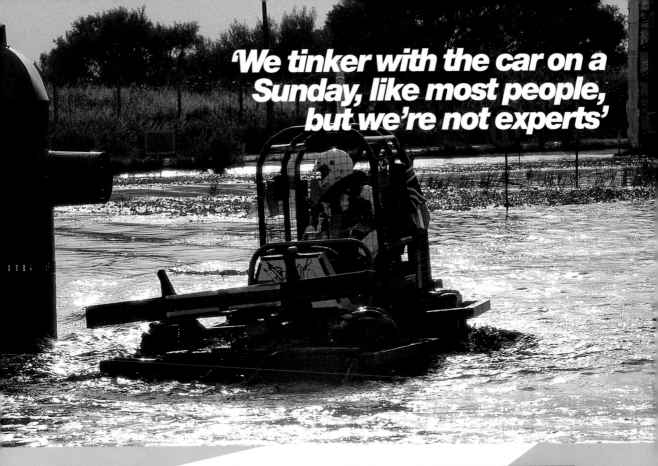

'We tinker with the car on a Sunday, like most people, but we're not experts'

Pure Adrenalin

DONOR VEHICLE
Four-wheel drive building site dumper

ENGINE TYPE
5.9cc GMC V8
250 bhp

TRANSMISSION TYPE
Automatic

ESTIMATED WEIGHT
2750 kg

OVERALL LENGTH
14 feet

WIDTH
7 feet 2 inches

HEIGHT
7 feet

SUSPENSION TYPE
Flat tyres/no suspension

FUEL TYPE
Petrol

OTHER FEATURES
Articulated chassis
Hydraulic steering

Toilet Humour

The team's Sealed Knot activities were a theme of the video they submitted to RDF in the hope of being accepted as contestants. In one of the funniest tapes RDF received, Hoppy, Acker and Magic each put on their helmets and declare, 'See you down the battle, lads!' but Magic discovers that his car has run out of diesel. Acker offers to siphon some out of his car, but after a while decides that getting a proper siphoning system would be easier. They know where to find a siphoning system, and promptly head for the nearest toilet. There follows a quick explanation of toilet technology (fulfilling one of RDF's prerequisites that each video should explain how something mechanical functions) before they finally get Magic's car started. The saga ends as Hoppy emerges from his house with a toilet under his arm!

The Bodysnatchers
Buckinghamshire, United Kingdom

Tim Miles

Although Debbie appears to be the dominant member of the team, Tim is in fact the captain. The 34-year-old is the team's youngest member, but has a wealth of experience: he is a former blacksmith and Land Rover garage mechanic who was a member of the Royal Engineers for ten years.

Debbie Bilton

A former accountant who has vowed never to return to office work, she is now a paramedic shift officer. She says, 'I have the perfect skills required to drive because I drive emergency vehicles for a living.' Debbie will be sharing the driving responsibilities with her fellow team-mates.

Gerry Lea

Gerry is the biggest, and quietest, member of The Bodysnatchers. An ex-Royal Marine and North Sea diver, Gerry has served in such diverse scenarios as the Falkland Islands and the Brixton Academy, where he worked as bouncer. 'I can do everything Tim can do,' he boasts, 'except I can do it underwater as well!'

'We don't like each other,' jokes The Bodysnatchers' Gerry. 'We just work together.' The Bodysnatchers are a team with more experience of putting people together than cars. The three paramedics are based at a busy station in Milton Keynes, and each works 12 hour shifts, so finding the time to construct their vehicle was especially difficult.

The team were only united in their workshop on three occasions during the four-week build. For the rest of the time they communicated by leaving phone messages for one another. There was extra pressure on single mum Debbie, who already had a week's holiday booked when the team were invited to take part in the competition. 'My children think it's great that I'm doing *Full Metal Challenge*, but I think they would have preferred it if I had been at home. On the days I'm off work I would normally do the shopping and the housework, but for three weeks I used that time to work on the vehicle until I had to pick the children up from school. As a result my garden's gone to pot and my house is a complete mess!'

Although she wasn't around all the time the vehicle was being built, Debbie played a crucial role in finding a donor car and a workshop in which to customise it. 'We wanted something that was quite small, agile and tough,' she says. 'Someone suggested a Ferret scout car to us, and we knew that could handle just about any terrain so we thought it would be ideal. We also knew it would be watertight, which we thought might come in useful. We designed around the Ferret and RDF loved it, although we didn't actually go with my original design.'

Why wasn't the original design adopted? 'Practicalities,' she says, listing the problems and setbacks. 'Lack of time, lack of sponsors...'

Debbie eventually sourced a Ferret from a dealer in Norfolk. 'They can be quite difficult to get hold of,' she says, 'because people have started to buy them and renovate them as a hobby, sometimes taking five years to do it.' The team set about adapting their purchase, which they christened

'we'll take the knocks
if we get any'

'We wanted something that was quite small, agile and tough'

Stomp, stripping away elements until they could bring the vehicle within the competition's weight restrictions. Did they feel any remorse or guilt over the way they were treating this armoured antique? 'Absolutely not!' says Debbie emphatically.

If The Bodysnatchers chose a relatively conventional way to create a vehicle, there was certainly nothing conventional about where they made it. Stomp came together at a workshop in Bletchley

Park, the once top secret facility where the Germans' Enigma code was cracked during the Second World War. The team were able to draw upon the facilities and the experience of Bletchley staff Gordon and Brian, who were experts in restoring military vehicles. On some days they were joined by Tim's five-year-old son, who proved to be an enthusiastic assistant.

'We've kept gimmicks and gadgets to a minimum,' says Tim. 'I'm quite glad about that, because I think some of the vehicles I've seen in the workshop here have been over-engineered. Apart from the armour on the front and the sides, we've kept ours simple. There are no axles to go wrong – it's all sub-axles and they're inside a completely moulded hull. Each wheel is driven by a separate prop shaft and we've got monstrously strong suspension. It's indestructible really. The only thing I can see giving us a problem will be low-speed manoeuvring.'

The Ferret had been standing idle for around 15 years before The Bodysnatchers breathed new life into it, and certain parts had not survived intact. The team's first trial run proved a little traumatic for the wildlife at Bletchley Park when, with Gerry behind the wheel, the throttle got stuck in the open position and the brakes failed. By the time Stomp was ready to be delivered to the site in Kent, the team worked out that they had only gone over-budget by approximately £50 each – and some of that could be put down to fuel costs.

The team's confidence can partly be explained by the fact that they were invited to take part in *Full Metal Challenge* because they were veterans of *Scrapheap Challenge* in 2000. 'We don't know what to expect from the courses,' says Gerry, 'but in some ways we feel like we're used to this.'

'We'll take the knocks, if we get any,' he continues. 'I've been looking at some of the other vehicles and they might seem to have the advantage over us, insofar as they've got power-steering or automatic gearboxes, but could they survive direct contact? We'll see.'

Ferreting Around

The Ferret armoured scout car was first developed by Daimler in late 1948, and almost 4500 Ferrets were built between 1952 and 1971. The British Army kept the Ferret in active service until the mid-1990s, but it is estimated that around a thousand are still being used in some of the 36 countries that placed orders for the vehicles. The Ferret was built to accommodate two men – usually a driver and a commander – but some models had their ammunition panniers replaced with collapsible seats in order to carry up to four people. The vehicle was armed with a .30 calibre Browning machine (which, as an offensive weapon, precludes it from *Full Metal Challenge*) and featured a Rolls-Royce engine weighing around 3.75 tons.

Diary Extracts

Day 1
Nightmare! Ferrets are about as common as rocking horse doo-dah!

Day 13
Half the battle is keeping everyone working without undoing what the previous person has done. It's difficult, with all of us working full time, to maintain a degree of continuity. For example, Debbie can do a lot of things but welding isn't one of them, so we've got to leave her plenty to get on with. It's a real discipline for Gerry and I not to do things!

Day 16
Set fire to the bin while using cutting torch. Dad can move pretty quick for a 67-year-old.

Day 18
Blasting holes through armour-plate is an exhilarating experience!
The flashbacks are incredible!

Day 22
Beefed up Debbie's front end – a most gratifying experience! The engine is making a strange noise – not unlike a load of nuts and bolts going around a washer/dryer on its spin cycle.

Day 27
Gerry spent an enjoyable day battling valiantly with the seat. It's finally all mounted up but it's hardly what you'd call comfortable – we'll be driving with our knees either side of our ears!

Day 28
The roll cage has arrived – hurrah!
It doesn't fit – boo!

Day 29
A storming day. Amazingly all of us were in the workshop. The cage is in, after Gerry's tweaking. Debbie's getting on with the bodywork – she's even painted it! We've gone for an aggressive-looking matt black. Should scare the opposition.

Stomp

DONOR VEHICLE
Daimler Ferret armoured scout car

ENGINE TYPE
Rolls-Royce waterproof engine 120 bhp

TRANSMISSION TYPE
Pre-select semi-automatic

ESTIMATED WEIGHT
3000 kg

OVERALL LENGTH
12 feet

WIDTH
6 feet

HEIGHT
7 feet 6 inches

SUSPENSION TYPE
Independent coil spring and wishbone, double-acting hydraulic

FUEL TYPE
Petrol

OTHER FEATURES
Four-wheel drive – individual drive shaft to each wheel

Chicago Fire
Chicago, USA

Mike Kappel

Team captain and driver Mike is a firefighter and garage-owner by profession. His wife gave birth to their fourth child shortly before work started on the team's vehicle. 'She wasn't very happy about me doing *Full Metal Challenge* but she went along with it,' he jokes. 'I got some rather dirty looks. She's got to be an angel to put up with a guy like me!'

Joseph Mrozek

Joe is an expert welder and mechanic who worked in the truck industry for 17 years before becoming a fireman. His hobbies include racing cars and bikes, and riding his 1986 Harley-Davidson. He is happy to let Mike take responsibility for the driving, but says, 'If Mike loses this competition for us, we're going to leave him in England!'

Edward Brennan (aka Proby)

Ed spent 16 years as a mechanic at Chevrolet before becoming a firefighter. He is the quietest member of the team, and enjoys relatively sedate hobbies such as golf and softball. He is nevertheless determined to do well: 'We didn't come over to the UK for nothing,' he says. 'We came here to win.'

Chicago Fire are a formidable trio of hard-bitten firefighters who are all veterans of *Junkyard Wars*. The team's vehicle is named 911, after the American emergency telephone number (the US equivalent of 999) and in tribute to the 11 September rescue workers. Team captain Mike was part of the rescue operation at Ground Zero following the attacks on the World Trade Center. 'I spent just over a week there,' he says, his eyes casting downwards. 'We lost 343 firefighters and it was hard being down there, digging for your brothers. If you want to say I was there then that's fine, but it's hard to talk about.'

911 dominates the *Full Metal Challenge* workshop, dwarfing many of the other vehicles. The design for this jacked-up monster truck was a joint effort, following some preliminary sketches by Joe. The donor chassis came from a 1979 Dodge Power Wagon. 'It was a piece of junk that had been rotting away in my mother-in-law's driveway for 13 years,' says Mike. 'She was glad to see it go!'

Ed is keen to point out that although Chicago Fire used a donor vehicle, their car was virtually scratch-built. 'It was really framed from a pick up truck but the whole thing was taken apart and almost everything was replaced, from the brake lines down to the last screw.'

Once the Dodge had been stripped down the team started work on the roll cage, which was an amended version of a design that RDF had rejected. 'We had trouble with that,' confirms Mike, a smouldering cigar clenched between his teeth. 'The bars going lengthways were fine but then we had bars coming off those at a 90 degree angle. If we had put those bars on and the car had fallen on someone then it would have killed them.' The team were instead asked to weld the side roll bars on at a 45 degree angle. Mike takes a moment to reflect on the change, before concluding that, 'If this thing falls on someone it's still going to kill them!'

911 was assembled at the workshop of Mike's auto repair business, but the team were divided by

'If this thing falls on someone it's still going to kill them!'

their firefighting shifts and geography – Mike and Ed work at the north end of the city and Joe works in the south, around 20 miles away. The three team-members were only united during the build for five of the 30 days. Mike is proud that, despite the obvious communication problems, the team managed to stay pretty much on budget. 'When we were building the car, if we needed something all three of us just went out and got it,' he recalls. 'We didn't really look at how much we were spending, so I had a friend of mine do a spreadsheet. He said, "You're only over by ten dollars!" Eventually we got even that down. We had no idea that we were that close – right on the line.'

'It came to $3006 and 50 cents,' adds Joe, 'so we split the six dollars and 50 cents between us!'

Testing 911 led to some major difficulties for Chicago Fire – the first of which was finding somewhere to unleash the behemoth. 'For us to have taken it off-road, we would have had to put it on a trailer and drive it 30 miles,' says Mike. 'It would have been a two-hour drive to take it to a country site. We had some major problems during the building and we were right up to the wire – there was just no time.'

The team had to content themselves with driving the vehicle up and down an alley a few times, but when they got to England they put the vehicle through a more vigorous last-minute test. Two days before the team were due to film their heat, they got a bit carried away and 911 went over a ridge at 30 miles per hour. Its brief flight came to an abrupt end with disastrous consequences. 'Bam!' says Mike, smacking his hands together to illustrate the crash. 'When it hit the ground, the cooling fan went right through the radiator. It was an all-day project trying to fix it, but in the end we got a new radiator.'

All three of them laugh out loud when asked whether the thought of competing in the first heat makes them nervous. 'We're used to pressure,' says Mike, who has been nominated to drive. 'When you walk into a burning building when everyone is running out – including rats, cockroaches and dogs – there has got to be something wrong with you!'

'That's the way it is,' agrees Joe. 'I'm curious about the other vehicles, but because of the situations we face every day we're prepared for anything. Nothing's going to shock us – that's just the way we are.'

'I've got great faith in Joe's welding skills,' says Mike. 'I know that nothing's going to stop us.

'I'm not worried about collisions,' he smiles, purposefully stubbing out his cigar. 'In fact, I'm kind of hoping for them!'

911

DONOR VEHICLE
Dodge Power Wagon

ENGINE TYPE
360 CID

TRANSMISSION TYPE
Automatic

SUSPENSION TYPE
Leaf spring

FUEL TYPE
Petrol

OTHER FEATURES
Four-wheel drive

Common Ground

The day before filming the Chicago Fire team took a break from tinkering with 911 to get some lunch at the location canteen. 'We just had lunch with Henry!' beamed Mike afterwards, who was pleased to discover that his team shared some common ground with the *Full Metal Challenge* co-presenter. 'He's a nice guy,' said Ed. 'We were talking about Chicago for quite a while. He told us he really likes it, and plays there quite a lot.'

Pitball
Aim of the game: push the flaming ball outside the ring of fire

Pitball is filmed inside one of the cooling towers after dark, and has a decidedly eerie feel about it. The game takes place on a circular pitch which is shaped like a flat-bottomed bowl. The sides of this bowl-like pit form a 30-degree gradient. At the top of the lip of the bowl, 30.5 metres in diameter, is a ring of fire. All three teams are on the pitch together. The game starts when a giant flaming ball is dropped into the field of play. The vehicles must head for the flaming ball in the centre of the pitch and, once they have made contact with it, do everything they can to keep possession. Once they have made contact with the ball, they must push it up the gradient and over the lip – through the ring of fire – in order to score a goal. Cameras watch their progress from the sides of the cooling tower and from above. This is a hair-raising test of the vehicles' speed, traction and manoeuvrability.

The Rules

A goal is scored by pushing the flaming ball outside the ring, denoted by a circle of fire. The ball must pass entirely outside the ring to score – a linesman will judge whether this is the case. The goal will be awarded to whichever team made the last physical contact with the ball before it went over the line.

The game will continue until one team has scored a goal. That team will be the winner of the game and then leave the pitch. The game will continue with two teams until one of them scores a goal.

At the point the second team scores a goal, the game ends. Even though this is a physical game, the global rule applies – namely that any team who drive in such a way as to disable another vehicle will be immediately removed from the pitch and disqualified from the game.

In the event that two vehicles are physically in contact with the ball at the time it passes outside the ring, the goal will not count, no points will be awarded and the ball will be relaunched.

Country Boys
North Carolina, USA

Keith Hartzog
Team captain and driver Keith is a former volunteer fireman, and has worked in law enforcement for 16 years. He is also a race shop owner, and shares his enthusiasm for motor sports with his whole family. 'My daughter is the only 12-year-old in the world who knows how to change a tyre properly,' he says proudly.

Brian Perkins (aka Corky)
Corky is a workshop owner and mechanic with 26 years of drag-racing experience. His father was also a mechanic, and as a youth he took part in potentially dangerous street races. 'We're a bunch of country boys who drink moonshine, race fast cars and chase all the women,' he says, laughing. 'I'm just a motorhead. I love it!'

Billy Stafford
Spare parts supplier Billy describes his role as 'junior mechanic and scavenger'. His hobbies include stock car racing, hunting and fishing, and his recent acquisitions include a new bass boat. 'I'm very good with my hands,' he says. 'I'm willing to get down and dirty for my team.'

The Country Boys, as their name suggests, are resourceful, cocksure Southerners with a sense of national identity quite different from many of their fellow Americans in the competition. Team captain Keith is a deputy sheriff and has known Corky for 19 years. Corky's imposing frame and slow-talking delivery make him seem like a modern-day John Wayne, although this is a cowboy who would be more comfortable with a spanner in his hand than a gun. Corky reveals that this is the first time he has ever left the East Coast, let alone the USA.

Joining Keith and Corky is Billy Stafford, who at 31 years old is the youngest member of the team by far. Billy rents his home from Corky, and the three men are all firm friends. Although they strenuously resist attempts to stereotype them as hard-living rednecks, they all seem to enjoy the lifestyle: barbeques, hunting, car-racing and the occasional beer. All except for Keith, that is, who doesn't drink. 'I do stupid enough things when I'm sober!' he laughs.

The Country Boys' vehicle, the Southern Crusher, is the only American tracked machine in the competition, although the team are quick to point out that the donor vehicle (a Bombardier snow plough) was Canadian and that they've either strengthened or rebuilt every single component.

'We aimed to create a machine that could go anywhere something with four wheels couldn't go,' says Keith, 'and I think we've pretty much done that.' Unfortunately, the unique nature of the vehicle's design and construction caused some unforeseen problems for the team, as Corky explains: 'The main component of our tracks is basically a large rubber band, four inches wide and half an inch thick. There are two on each side, and we couldn't find a source for new ones. The Bombardier is out of production now, and we could only find one guy who sold the parts we needed, so we had to pay his price. We spent half of our money on rubber bands, and went over budget as a result.'

'We already feel like winners because we got chosen'

The tracks had already caused the team a problem with RDF, who were concerned that the steel cleats might damage the floors of some of the sets. The team tried to attach three different types of rubber blocks to the tracks before they found something that fitted.

Was there anything else RDF objected to on their original design? 'Yeah,' says Corky. 'They wouldn't let us put a gun on it.'

As the filming date approached, the team expressed concerns about the potential weak spots of their vehicle. 'I hope we don't have problems with the tracks,' said Brian, while Corky had reservations about another of the vehicle's rubber components. 'We've checked out some of the other vehicles, and they use a steel gear. Ours is a giant rubber gear, and we're concerned that it

might get chewed up. The manufacturer told us that would only happen if it had age on it, but we've got a much more powerful engine on this – something like 350 horsepower.'

'I could take this thing up to 60 kph,' says Brian, nodding, 'but I would only do 45 because I think anything more would put too much stress on the rubber tracks. One good thing about the tracks, however, is that we're not worried what the weather's going to be like when we're filming. It can rain, sleet or snow – the only surface that would give us problems would be a super-smooth concrete floor. If it was too slick we'd slide around on it.'

While they were in the workshop, The Country Boys spent some time with the other teams, and were naturally intrigued by The Snowdiggers'

tracked vehicle, the Steel Survivor. 'They used the tracks of a big snowmobile,' says Billy, 'but I think they've built their vehicle too big. All the teams are fun, they're real great people. The Australians [The Flamin' Aussies] are real serious about it – it's not fun to them. It's like, if they don't win they can't go home! They're all female and they're trying to get into what is generally considered a male area, so I guess I can understand the way they feel.'

Aside from the aforementioned problems, the build period for the Southern Crusher was typically laid back. 'We used Keith's workshop, which was a big help,' says Billy. 'In this country, when you finish work you go the pub. When we finished work we'd stop off at the convenience store, buy a big pack of beers, go over to Keith's and put them in the cooler. We'd work on the vehicle in the evenings, and if

anyone wanted to stop by and help us then we let them help us with the beer as well. During the last week, we got everyone who'd picked up a tool to sign the machine. We even got the sheriff to sign it!'

Billy has a clear strategy for success when the Southern Crusher goes before the cameras. 'Our concern is the course, not the machine. Keith will be taking it nice and slow – we want him to ease into it little by little and work his way up. He's had a lot of experience – we feel we've got the right driver.'

'If anything goes wrong it's going to pretty much fall on the driver,' says Corky. 'We built it to be the very best there is, so if anything goes wrong it'll be because of driver error.'

'They planned it all this way,' laughs Keith, 'so if anything happens they can blame it all on me!'

'If anything goes wrong it'll be because of driver error'

Diary Extracts

Day 2
Cut away scrap steel and ordered track bands from Canada.

Day 3
Sand blast, sand blast, sand blast. Placed corpse on stretcher and wheeled it into the operating theatre. We are tired and dirty. The shop looks like a beach from all this sand.

Day 4
We are happy, but Billy is sad, so we gave him a deck chair and a beach ball.

Day 5
Drove over 300 miles and visited five salvage yards but eventually found transmission core.

Day 23
Short tempers.

Day 26
Tested machine - power from Hell!

Day 29
Finished most of machine. Too tired to write any more.

Day 30
A lot of ideas have been left on the drawing board. We really wanted to get a couple of outriggers on board but ran out of time. Tested late in the day - nothing fell off so we called it 'mission accomplished'. Glad it's over.

Southern Crusher Mark II

'We have done a lot to get here,' says Billy, 'and we already feel like winners because we got chosen.' In fact, The Country Boys feel so good about the *Full Metal Challenge* experience that they have already resolved to build another vehicle, this time for their own amusement. 'We do a lot of hunting,' Billy continues, 'and a vehicle like this would be good for getting through rough terrain in woods. There'll be some things we do differently on ours – we won't need to make it quite so smash-proof.' The three friends are currently looking for a donor vehicle to convert, and Corky is already enthused about the possibilities: 'Whatever we do, it's gonna be real beautiful.'

Southern Crusher

DONOR VEHICLE
Bombardier snow plough

ENGINE TYPE
Chevy V8
350 bhp

TRANSMISSION TYPE
GM turbo 400 bolt-on yoke

ESTIMATED WEIGHT
4900 kg

OVERALL LENGTH
10 feet

WIDTH
5 feet 5 inches

HEIGHT
6 feet

SUSPENSION TYPE
Spring-loaded

FUEL TYPE
Petrol

OTHER FEATURES
Tracks – steers by braking on selected side

The Death Guild

San Francisco, USA

Sam Nordemann

Team captain Sam is a graphic designer whose experiences with the Californian underground have seen him build a geodesic dome, work on a bungee jump and stage *Mad Max*-style battles. Most of his mechanical knowledge comes from his passion for amateur motorbike racing and off-roading.

Mathew Noble

Mathew is a bar-tender and bouncer with an impressive collection of firearms – none of which we hope he takes to work! His hobbies include taking part in pistol competitions, martial arts, auto-cross and rally-driving.

David Howe (aka Big Dave)

Man mountain Big Dave is a night club bouncer and airsmith - ie someone who specialises in designing and making paintball guns. His hobbies include racing cars and motorbikes, and he has been designated the team's chief engineer. 'We're very democratic though,' he stresses. 'We all try to have a little artistic input.'

From the melting pot of San Francisco's sub-culture comes The Death Guild. Mathew and Sam's style is a collision between Goth and that 'ridden off the range' look (remember Fields of the Nephilim, anyone?). And Big Dave... has probably the most appropriate nickname of anyone in the competition. All three are *Mad Max* fans, and everything about their attitude and their vehicle shows that they are clearly living the dream.

These nocturnal road warriors seem ill-at-ease in the glaring sunlight of the *Full Metal Challenge* site, and Mathew confirms that they were partly selected because of their appearance. 'I think the hardest part of this whole thing so far was getting chosen,' he says. 'When I asked them why they picked us they said it was because we were interesting-looking.'

The three friends heard about *Full Metal Challenge* from an acquaintance, and logged on to the website that contained details of the entrance procedure. They chose the name Death Guild after the club where Big Dave works as a bouncer and started to prepare their video. 'We built a catapult in the street,' says Sam, 'and filmed ourselves putting it together, explaining what we were doing. We got ten shots out of it in the end. We were just glad it worked!'

The team's vehicle is called Monkey – a name that caused some confusion with the show's producers. 'They were confused because they thought of a monkey as a little critter that runs around, whereas we use the word monkey as a way of describing how you make something work. We've been arguing with them over this ever since.'

Sam, Mathew and Big Dave have already constructed vehicles for their own amusement. Previous efforts have included such dubious accessories as flame-throwers and propane torches. The rules banning offensive weapons precluded any such nastiness in *Full Metal Challenge*, but the team were still determined that Monkey would mean business. 'We went shopping

'We needed a good motor on a strong chassis at a cheap price and that's what we got'

for a vehicle to convert,' remembers Mathew, 'and we eventually found a 1977 Chevy Blazer. We needed a good motor on a strong chassis at a cheap price and that's what we got. We spent the majority of the money and then some on making it more rugged. We were lucky with the roll cage because we got a lot of free metal donated to us.'

RDF initially objected to the team using a nose section culled from a trailer truck. 'We wanted to use this big front end but they told us we couldn't because they were worried that it might burn,' says Mathew.

'I know you don't have things like that over here,' says Sam, 'but we thought this was ridiculous because they're used in drag racing all the time at home. Anyway, we had already gotten rid of it by the time they came back to us and said that it was actually OK. The whole thing sent us over budget.'

'We felt frustrated because it seemed the rules kept changing,' says Mathew, 'but when I mentioned this to one of the producers he reminded me that this was the first time they had put on a show like this and I could understand that. They didn't have anything to measure against – we were the experiment.'

'We haven't seen much of the course,' adds Big Dave, 'but what we have seen glimpses of has surprised us. We expected the courses to be much

more industrial, because of the name of the show. It's interesting that the courses have been designed to be more like movie sets.'

The only other major change to the design of Monkey was the armour which the team planned to put over the wheels. 'We were worried that the armour might make it difficult for us to manoeuvre through a gap so we scrapped it,' says Mathew. 'We were going to make most of the armour we put on there removable, but in the end we decided it wasn't worth the effort and we were running out of time anyway.'

'The bumpers and the tyres are the strongest part of the vehicle,' he continues. 'In fact the whole thing's really strong – a front or rear collision won't be a problem.'

'Side collisions could be difficult,' says Big Dave. 'The front wheels are wide open. If something bangs into them real hard it will damage a wheel rod or an axle.'

The team tossed a coin to decide who would be captain, and are similarly laid back about who will be handling the driving. One thing they are all agreed on, however, is that no one is keen to tackle The Hall of Mirrors game: 'It's because the vehicle's so wide,' says Big Dave. 'We can't make it any narrower, but if we need to take it anywhere where there are tight corners then it's going to be difficult!'

Monkey

DONOR VEHICLE
1977 Chevy Blazer

ENGINE TYPE
400 small block

TRANSMISSION TYPE
Turbo 400

ESTIMATED WEIGHT
2400 kg

OVERALL LENGTH
15 feet

WIDTH
7 feet 4 inches

HEIGHT
7 feet 6 inches

SUSPENSION TYPE
Leaf spring and shock absorbers

FUEL TYPE
Petrol

OTHER FEATURES
Four-wheel drive, 35 inch foam-filled tyres

Sunday Drivers

Finding places to effectively test vehicles was a big problem for contestants working in urban areas, but The Death Guild came up with a novel solution. 'There were a lot of construction sites near us,' says Mathew, 'and these were never very busy on Sundays. We'd take the vehicle to these places on Sunday afternoons, when there was no one else around.'

'The testing was useful,' says Sam. 'We found out that Monkey handled well, and we were able to work out the build-up time for the momentum. It is a little lighter at the back, but we already knew about that and there's nothing we can do about it now. We're all used to driving rear-geared vehicles.'

The Desert Pumas
Iquique, Chile

Attilio Gattavara Ghillino

Genial team captain Attilio is a successful industrialist with his own polystyrene factory. He began working on cars when he was 16 and studied engineering at university before starting a mining business. He is a popular figure: 'Everyone knows me and likes me!' he smiles.

Pedro Lazaro Boari

An architect by trade, Pedro was the Secretary of Regional Planning after the demise of General Pinochet. He met Attilio when he moved to Iquique in 2001, and shortly afterwards designed his new factory.

Nestor Aguilera

Nestor grew up around cars (his father had a trucking business) and learned to weld when aged just 11. He studied metallurgy at university but decided instead to pursue a career as a mechanic. He helps maintain Attilio's collection of off-road vehicles and says, 'I may look innocent, but really I'm a trickster.'

Although only team captain Attilio has good grasp of English, it is clear that there is nothing frivolous about the Chilean team. These distinguished gentlemen are led by the patriarchal Attilio, whose strong, sonorous voice seems to silence all debate with admirable ease. The three friends are amongst the more mature contestants (Nestor is 46, Attilio and Pedro are 57) and seem to be approaching the competition with all the seriousness of a military campaign.

Speaking through an interpreter, the team-mates are passionate about their home town of Iquique (located in one of the driest regions in the world) and keen to express how much *Full Metal Challenge* means to them.

'I describe myself as a poet of the desert,' says the ever-smiling Pedro. 'I like to write poetry and music and I find that the desert inspires me. I'm proud that we have made it this far, and it would make me happy to think that we can inspire other people to do the same thing, especially young people.'

All three are professionals with responsibilities, but they came together through their boyish enthusiasm for tinkering with cars and off-roading. Attilio is especially proud of his personal collection of four-wheel drive jeeps - six in total - and clearly applies the same cool determination to his hobby as his business enterprises.

'There was not enough money to create the vehicle I designed,' says Attilio, describing the remarkable Marabunta. 'I know that we used every spare moment we had to build it, but I don't know exactly how much money we had to contribute ourselves. That was never the most important thing for us - the most important thing was simply to come here and compete.'

The Marabunta was named after an indigenous insect. 'It's a small creature that eats everything in sight,' explains Attilio. 'It's a real fighter as well. They work in groups, like soldier ants.'

The Marabunta is a unique and ingenious design.

'We've got a very good vehicle, but more importantly we've got three very good drivers'

'I'm proud that we have made it this far, and it would make me happy to think that we can inspire other people to do the same thing'

The vehicle uses a front-wheel drive transaxle mounted sideways to power a front and rear differential. The front wheels steer in the traditional way, but the back wheels can also be turned, meaning the vehicle is able to steer in any configuration. The result is a highly agile and easy-to-manoeuvre vehicle with an impressive power-to-weight ratio.

Attilio proudly explains that his team chose to compete 'the difficult way. I've looked at many cars here, and a lot of people have adapted other vehicles. We didn't want to do that. We bought a used Mitsubishi engine and a gearbox, but we constructed the vehicle from scratch. There was an extra problem for us, because although we were originally given 30 days to build the car we only actually had 26. We had to meet the date when the car was due to be exported to England, and this fell four days before the end of our original schedule.'

When asked if the team had any time to test the vehicle in Iquique Nestor just laughs. 'We had four minutes! Luckily it works very well - we've got no problems at all. The only thing that might give us a problem is deep water - I don't think the car will work if it is submerged too deep.'

The Desert Pumas feel an extra burden of responsibility because of their strong sense of national pride. 'It's not just that we're the only team from Chile,' says Nestor. 'We're very much aware that we're the only team from South America, so we feel we're representing Iquique, we're representing Chile, and we're representing the whole continent.'

'We're not worried about anything though,' says Attilio. 'We've got a very good vehicle, but more importantly we've got three very good drivers. The rules are going to prevent this from becoming a demolition derby, so we suspect that the winners will be the most skilful drivers. We don't know who will be driving in our heat - we'll decide when we get a chance to examine the courses, but we all have different skills and we will apply them in the most effective way. We've enjoyed everything about this experience so far and we're going to keep on enjoying it.'

Diary Extracts

Day 1
We purchased two axles, the engine and some pipes. All hands to the job!

Day 2
We begin work on the structure by cutting, bending and welding pipes for the chassis.

Day 5
The chassis is even stronger than we anticipated. We are now sure we made the right decision in creating something from scratch.

Day 9
Once again, the electrics are proving to be the most problematic area.

Day 11
Fixed engine to chassis.

Day 15
Broadened the wheels and installed the vertical body structure.

Day 17
Tested the engine - it started and is running!

Day 25
Final fixing of axles and suspension.

Day 26
Installed pedals and brake lines.
We're ready!

Marabunta

DONOR VEHICLE
None

ENGINE TYPE
V6 2.5 litre

TRANSMISSION TYPE
Automatic

ESTIMATED WEIGHT
1500 kg

OVERALL LENGTH
11 feet 8 inches

WIDTH
6 feet 2 inches

SUSPENSION TYPE
Spring-loaded

FUEL TYPE
Petrol

OTHER FEATURES
Four-wheel drive

Hall of Mirrors
Aim of the game: drive to the centre of the maze and back out again as quickly as possible

Hall of Mirrors takes place in a maze nearly 60 metres in diameter. The walls of the maze are made of distorting mirrors of the type you might find at a fairground. Inside the maze are nine moving turnstiles, which rotate through 120 degrees changing the route through the maze for a passing vehicle.

All three team vehicles enter the maze at the same time at symmetrical points on the outside. They must head for the centre of the maze and then return as quickly as possible in order to win. Each 120 degree segment of the maze is identical, so no team has an unfair advantage over another. The nine gates are rotating units which, by moving through 120 degrees, will close off a previously open route, or open up a previously closed one. It will be impossible to reach the centre without passing through at least two of these gates. The gates rotate through 120 degrees in one direction every time a vehicle passes through them.

Cameras look down on the cars from towers that loom over the maze. The watching team-members will be able to see a monitor, which shows an overhead shot of the maze. They will be in communication with the driver and are allowed and encouraged to give advice on the best route in and out of the maze.

This is a fiendishly frustrating test of the cars' speed and manoeuvrability.

The Rules

Details of the gate rotation shall not be made known to the teams.
The maze is divided into hexagonal 'cells'. If a team is within a cell, it is theirs and no other team has the right to enter that cell.
No passing is allowed within a cell.
In the event that two or more teams are competing to get into the same cell, the referees will judge who was there first.
The winner is the team who makes it back out to the outside first, irrespective of who was the first to the centre position. Similarly, second place goes to the second team out.

The Dodgy Oppos
Devon, United Kingdom

Anthony Edwards (aka Nutty)
Team captain Nutty has been in the Marines for 22 years – he joined, aged 17, after taking shelter in a recruitment office during a rain storm. He has excellent fabrication and welding skills ('I could weld the crack of dawn!') and taught welding for four years.

Kevan Noble (aka Nobby)
Nobby has been in the Marines for 19 years, most of which he has spent specialising in equipment support for weapons, boats and vehicles. He is sport-obsessed and has represented the Marines at rugby, cricket and swimming.

David Davies (aka Windsor)
Windsor has been a Marine for 24 years and, like Nutty, served in the Falklands War. His hobbies include shooting, sub-aqua diving, hillwalking, car restoration and off-road racing. He recently inspired his nephew to join the Marines.

Nutty, Nobby and Windsor – The Dodgy Oppos – formed a close bond over decades of defending Queen and Country. Their team name means 'good companions', and they have travelled all over the world together, repairing military vehicles, often without proper tools, equipment or spare parts. They bring the same resourcefulness to *Full Metal Challenge*, rejecting the more extravagant approach adopted by certain other teams.

'We did go over budget,' says Nutty, 'but only by about forty quid. We thought the whole point of the competition was to try to stay on budget – we didn't want to put any of our own money in because we thought the point of the competition was to try and keep within the budget we'd been given.

'That aside, we're also tight!' he says, laughing.

Nutty stresses that the team's professional experience is thanks to the Royal Marines' philosophy that its front-line staff should all train in a relevant discipline. 'We're all tradesmen as well,' he says. 'I'm a fabricating welder, and Windsor and Knobby are both mechanics.'

The team constructed their vehicle, the Wolverine, at the workshops of the Commando Training Centre in Lympstone. 'We didn't ask for any financial help,' says Windsor, 'but we went to the planning office and they offered us the use of the workshop for free. I think it was a public relations trade-off.'

'We all chipped in to the design,' continues Windsor. 'The first design we submitted to RDF was based on a shortened Land Rover, but they thought that was crap! I think they liked the team, but didn't like our design – I think they'd had a lot of Land Rover designs already. So they wrote back to us and asked us if were interested in coming up with something else. It was a good thing really; looking back on it, a Land Rover would have been too easy.'

The design that was eventually accepted was based on the chassis from a four-wheel drive dirt dumper truck. The Wolverine has a two litre

'We decided to get
a cheap-as-chips
vehicle and armour it
to the teeth'

'We thought the point of the competition was to try and keep within the budget we'd been given'

engine, hydraulic steering and steel armour plating. 'We're guessing that speed will not be of the essence here,' says Windsor, 'so we decided to get a cheap-as-chips vehicle and armour it to the teeth.'

'It really is a simple design,' says Nutty. 'The dumper cost £1100, and I was concerned about spending that much because that was over half our budget gone. The next most expensive thing was the roll cage, which cost about £400. That's the only other thing we got from an external source, but we did all the welding ourselves.'

Although they admit to making a slow start ('Nutty: 'At the beginning I don't think we realised how much we had to get done in 30 days') they say that as work progressed they got faster. 'When I spoke to the officer about getting the workshop we pretty much told him that we'd do it in our own time,' says Knobby, 'but as it progressed that got harder. A lot of time was spent going to companies looking for things, most of which we couldn't use because they asked for some publicity in return.'

'You can't guarantee time off in our jobs,' says Windsor. 'We worked on it a lot during the day, stayed late a few nights and on Wednesdays, when we normally get time off for sport, we worked on the vehicle instead. We're used to working to deadlines – after all, you can't tell someone, "Can you put your war off for a while? We're not ready yet."'

The team removed the truck's arms and dumper and, as work continued, complied with RDF's request that the fuel tank be put in a specific place. 'Our fuel pump's going to be working overtime because of where they've asked us to put the tank,' says Nobby. 'I would have preferred to have put it in the engine compartment, but they wanted us to move it for health and safety reasons.'

The hydraulics have been preserved from the original vehicle, and any materials needed for maintenance were provided at cost price by a local company. When the ride-by was moved the team were lucky to be given extended hoses and pipes. There wasn't much time to test the vehicle, but when the RDF camera crew arrived to film the vehicle on its last build day they were pleasantly surprised to find that work was actually finished. 'Dan, the cameraman, couldn't believe it,' says Nobby. 'He said that with some of the other cars he'd filmed on their last days there were six or seven guys buzzing around trying to get the thing finished.'

The Wolverine's top speed is a modest 19 mph but, as Nutty knows from experience, when you hit a kerb at 19 mph without any suspension you certainly feel the impact. 'We've taken a lot of weight off the front,' he says, 'so it is a little bit back-heavy. If there's a ramming-type game and the other vehicles pick on us then we'll have to get away. The vehicle's got a ram, but if that gets damaged we could still carry on. One of my concerns is that the fuel cells are a bit exposed but we'll see what happens.'

'I don't know what I'm most nervous about,' says Nutty, who has been nominated to be the team's driver. 'I want to look good on camera,' he laughs, 'so I think I'll be most worried about my make-up, and keeping the swearing under control if we get rammed!'

Wolverine

DONOR VEHICLE
Bedford dumper

ENGINE TYPE
2.5 litre lifter

TRANSMISSION TYPE
Manual

ESTIMATED WEIGHT
2000 kg

OVERALL LENGTH
10 feet

WIDTH
7 feet

HEIGHT
7 feet

SUSPENSION TYPE
None

FUEL TYPE
Diesel

OTHER FEATURES
Four-wheel drive, articulated hydraulic steering

The Flamin' Aussies
Queensland, Australia

Melissa Thompson
'I've been into cars for as long as I can remember,' says team captain and driver Melissa, whose father builds race engines. Mel is a Christian, and her hobbies include racing a 506i big block dragster, skiing, water-skiing, horse riding and touch football.

Jane Casos
22-year-old Jane is the youngest member of the team. She was recently frustrated in her attempts to get a mechanic apprenticeship and laments the fact that it's difficult to be taken seriously. She has good welding skills and is currently building her own dragster.

Rebecca Anderson
Rebecca is an advisor at a service station and enjoys racing and restoring cars. She is now so proficient that she recently rebuilt a VF Valiant. She is very excited about competing in *Full Metal Challenge*: 'I've been waiting my whole life to do something like this!' she exclaims.

The Flamin' Aussies are the only all-female team, and three of only four women taking part in the whole contest. They positively bristle when questioned about what it feels like competing in the testosterone-fuelled environment of the *Full Metal Challenge* site, and are clearly determined to rise above both the competition and any chauvinism.

'The other teams have been great to us,' says Rebecca. 'They don't want us to fail, not just because we're women, but because they want competition themselves. If we fail then they've got less to compete against. We're over the whole gender thing. We're not trying to prove anything for women; we're not trying to prove that we're as good as men. If we'd been on a team with blokes we wouldn't have felt any different about this. We just want to compete – we're not here because we're feminists.'

'We're all involved in motor sports back in Australia so we have to deal with this all the time,' says Melissa. 'If they'd sent over three girls who'd never had to deal with that then they might have reacted badly to some of the comments we've been getting. On the whole, we just let it go.'

Perhaps unsurprisingly, The Flamin' Aussies are one of the most serious-minded teams. Unlike every other *Full Metal Challenge* team, these three contestants didn't know each other at all before the competition, and were specially selected to take part by the Australian Women's Motorsport Network. 'They short listed 300 girls which they thought would be good for a team, and it eventually came down to us three,' says Melissa. Bringing three strangers together caused some problems, as she explains. 'Jane and Rebecca are from Brisbane and I'm from the Big City, Sydney. So I was 12 hours' drive away from them. It made it difficult for all three of us to come together. When we were building the car I had to live in a tent for two-and-a-half weeks.'

The Flamin' Aussies describe themselves as 'car-mad hoons', which Jane explains is Australian

'We're over the whole gender thing'

'When we were building the car I had to live in a tent for two-and-a-half weeks'

'I couldn't find a strong enough engine, so I decided to use two and combine their power'

Flying Horse

DONOR VEHICLE
Two Beijing jeeps

ENGINE TYPE
2 4-cylinder jeep engines

TRANSMISSION TYPE
Manual

ESTIMATED WEIGHT
2400 kg

OVERALL LENGTH
17 feet 7 inches

WIDTH
7 feet 2 inches

HEIGHT
7 feet 2 inches

SUSPENSION TYPE
Leaf spring

FUEL TYPE
Petrol

OTHER FEATURES
Six-wheel drive

made these ourselves and got the remaining bits we needed to finish the vehicle off in England at the last minute.'

The cost of the two jeeps sent the budget way beyond the money allocated to the team. The final cost of the vehicle was an astronomical 15,000 US dollars, making it the most expensive vehicle in the whole competition. Tian and Guo-feng contributed what they could (Tian's girlfriend gave him $2000) but Zhong-qi ended up re-mortgaging his house in order to raise the remainder. 'If we hadn't done that we couldn't have finished the car before the deadline,' he says. 'My wife has been very understanding – I'm very grateful to her.'

Xing Ali, who is busy recording our exchange for China Central Television, takes a moment to put the team's financial sacrifices in context. 'I first heard about the team when I read about them in a newspaper,' she says. 'I was surprised they were able to compete at all because in China they would be considered peasants, and this has taken a very large amount of money. This is a very special event for them, and I thought it would make a good subject for a documentary. I want to record their excitement, happiness and joy. They're going to be

stars when they get home!'

There is not much happiness and joy coming from co-drivers Tian and Guo-feng, who look apprehensive about the competition, despite the fact they claim their testing period went well. 'We are confident,' insists Tian, who in all fairness seems more bamboozled by the media attention and the foreign country than the task ahead. 'The engines are strong and they can share the work. The front fender can move objects around and also gives us good protection. If there is a weakness then it could be in the limited flexibility, because the vehicle is so long; manoeuvrability might be hard. When we see the courses we will decide at the beginning of each one whether it will require a lot of manoeuvrability. If it does, we'll just unlock the rear end of the vehicle and take it away. That way we can turn a potential weakness into a potential strength.'

'I'm not concerned by all the attention we're getting,' says Zhong-qi. 'In fact I think that it's a spiritual benefit to us. This is a personal challenge to us, but we're aware that we're the only team from China. Whatever happens in the competition, I hope we have represented China's hardworking and devoted people.'

'We can turn a
potential weakness
into a potential strength'

Bumper Cars

Aim of the game: score the maximum number of points by hitting different static obstacles when they are lit up

Bumper Cars takes place on a circular arena at the base of one of the cooling towers. The arena is 40 metres in diameter and contains ten obstacles, five large and five small.

All three vehicles will be on the pitch together. Each team competes to hit as many obstacles as possible when they are lit. The more obstacles they hit, the more points they receive.

Points are only scored for hitting obstacles when they are lit up. Large obstacles score 50 points, small obstacles score 20. The central obstacle is merely decorative – it does not light up and does not score any points. The bumpers light up at pre-determined intervals that are unknown to the drivers.

Cameras watch their progress from the sides of the cooling tower and from above. This is a test of the vehicles' speed and manoeuvrability.

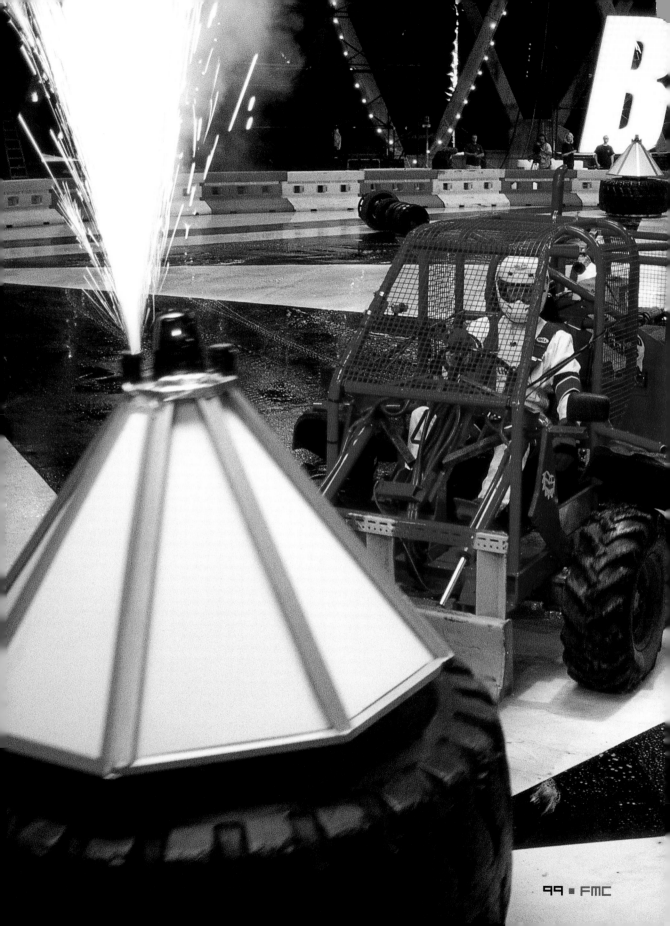

The Rules

Obstacles are lit up in a pre-determined sequence, which will not be revealed to the teams. They will be told, however, that small obstacles light up more often and stay lit up for longer than the larger obstacles.
In the event of a tie, the points will be split, ie for first/second/third place. A referee assigned to each team will be the sole judge of whether a vehicle scored a hit. The watching team-members will be able to see the scores on a monitor.

BUMPE

The Have A Go Likelies
East Sussex, United Kingdom

Barry Babister (aka Baz)
Team captain Baz has been fixing motorbikes and tractors since he was 12, and now owns a garage/MOT/recovery business in Hove. He was a stock car racing champion in 1999 and shares his passion for banger racing with his team-mates.

Stuart White (aka Big Stu)
For Stuart's eighth birthday his father gave him a car and told him to replace the clutch. He says he's been a mechanic ever since, and now co-owns three garage businesses with Baz. He met Baz at play school and the pair continue to pursue laddish pursuits such as skydiving, snowboarding and skiing.

Neil Challice
Former tree surgeon Neil now has his own landscape gardening business. He describes himself as the junior mechanic of the team – 'I'm the grafter,' he says, 'the blagger of spare parts.' As well as banger racing, his hobbies include Land Rover trials, off-road racing bikes and enduros.

The ebullient Have A Go Likelies originally applied to take part in *Scrapheap Challenge* and got down to the last 20 but weren't ultimately chosen. RDF didn't forget about them, however, and when preparations for *Full Metal Challenge* began the team were contacted and asked if they'd like to take part.

'We didn't have much to do,' recalls Neil, 'because we'd already done a video for the *Scrapheap Challenge* application. We submitted a sketch of our proposed vehicle, but I must admit I didn't think we'd ever get chosen. I think it's been harder for British teams to get into *Full Metal Challenge* than it has been for anyone else because of where we're from – more British people applied than any other nationality so there was more competition.'

Neil was worrying unnecessarily – The Have A Go Likelies and their vehicle, the Devil's Mule, were one of the later teams to be accepted and were soon given a whole new set of problems to worry about.

'Making a vehicle was nothing new for us,' says Neil, 'because we've been making cars for banger racing for years. We decided for this, however, to play the game properly and try to stick to the budget they'd given us. It wasn't easy.'

'We worked out the design together,' says Baz. 'Someone came up with the idea of using a dumper truck and we all thought this was quite appealing because of the vehicle's strength. There's nothing gimmicky about what we've done at all. We read the spec, which said that some pushing would be involved, and decided to build around that. Ours isn't a vehicle that will make you think "Wow" when you look at it, but I think it's basically indestructible. We could have added more, but there just wasn't time.'

The team bought the site dumper for £500. It had no engine or gearbox, so one of the first steps was to transplant those two essential components from a Ford Granada. They replaced the dumper's hydraulic bucket with a hydraulic bumper for extra protection and added pushing power.

'Ours isn't a vehicle that will make you think "Wow" when you look at it, but I think it's basically indestructible'

'We spent the other £1500 in the workshop, buying steel and other bits and pieces for the welding,' says Neil. 'About £150 of that went on the hydraulics and the hydraulic pump. By the time we'd finished we'd just skirted around the £2000 limit.'

'Midway through the build we had a testing day and blew up the transfer box,' says Stuart. 'We had to take it back to the workshop and tinker with the transmission box. Up until then we'd been £400 under budget, but time was running out so we decided to replace the damaged component. We had no choice but to buy another one – that came to the best part of £500.'

'In some ways that was a good thing,' says Neil. 'We've now got a reconditioned transmission box. Before we replaced it we could manage about 20 mph. Now we've got this automatic gearbox we can make 20 mph in first gear. We don't know how fast the vehicle can actually go, but on paper it should be able to reach 80 mph. Mind you, I think it would take quite a time to get there!'

Barry stresses that the Devil's Mule wasn't conceived with speed in mind. 'It was built to have contact with other vehicles. If anyone rams into it they will get damaged, and that's not because of any armour we've put on – it's because the vehicle's so strong. The axles each weigh three-quarters of a ton and are built to withstand a huge weight. There's no suspension, and I'm quite glad about that because I know other teams have been let down by their suspension. Ours hasn't got any so there's no way it can get damaged.'

The team have been impressed by many of the rival vehicles they've seen in the workshop, but critical of what they feel are overly elaborate designs. 'The Land Rover team [The Mud Hatters] look like they've made a vehicle for a lunar landing,' says Baz. 'I think what they really needed was a vehicle that could knock a building over.'

'We're bound to be nervous when we're out there,' says Stuart, who is sharing the driving with his team-mates, 'but if something goes wrong then we've got three good brains so we'll be able to fix it.'

'We've done a lot of racing,' says Baz, 'and you're nervous as hell when you first go out on the grid. This is something different, but it still feels a bit like racing.'

'The disaster would be if *Full Metal Challenge* was shown at 2.00 am when no one was watching,' says Stuart, laughing. 'We want to represent Britain, but it's also important to get on TV!'

Devil's Mule

DONOR VEHICLE
Winget dumper truck

ENGINE TYPE
Ford V6
130 bhp

TRANSMISSION TYPE
Automatic

ESTIMATED WEIGHT
2500 kg

OVERALL LENGTH
14 feet

WIDTH
6 feet

HEIGHT
6 feet 6 inches

SUSPENSION TYPE
None

FUEL TYPE
Petrol

OTHER FEATURES
Four-wheel drive
Dozer blade at front

The Hot Rods
California, USA

John Streets

Team captain John is 69, and not ashamed to admit he's the oldest contestant in the competition. John was born in Lincolnshire and served an engineering apprenticeship in the RAF before he emigrated to the US aged 21. He started his own company, Merlin Engineering, in 1969, but now pursues his motor sport hobbies full time.

Jay Streets

Jay is one of John's three sons, and was recruited primarily to be the team's driver. 42-year-old Jay has been racing since he was 13, and now competes professionally in tournaments. 'We each bring a different element to the table,' he says. 'I'm the test driver for all their ideas, that's my strength.'

John Buddenbaum

John is a self-employed fabricator and racing car restorer who is proud to have raced on the Silverstone track in the UK. In the US he has ranked as one of the top ten drivers in the Formula Ford racing league and has walked away unscathed from some horrendous accidents.

Generally speaking, the American *Full Metal Challenge* contestants are the most media-savvy; they know that the competitors are also required to be television performers, and most of them oblige with outlandish vehicles and personas. Nobody understands this better than The Hot Rods, vintage car enthusiasts who come with their own media pack, which includes a colourful press release, their own trading cards and enamel badges.

The Hot Rods' remarkable vehicle, the Double Dubb, employs two sets of engine / transmission / drive trains from a pair of Volkswagen Bugs, integrated into a custom frame which is hinged in the centre. Either or both engines can be used, and the hydraulically-operated centre steering adds to the vehicle's manoeuvrability.

'We found out about *Full Metal Challenge* on the internet,' says John B,' and by the time we found out the deadline to get the video applications in was only three days away so we had to work quickly.'

John S takes up the story: 'We have a friend called Dave Willis. He's a good graphic designer; John has done a lot of work with him. Dave helped us enormously: he gave us the first sketches and suggested a theme for what we should do. From there, we built a full-size mock-up.'

'From the very beginning the idea was to sell them a strange vehicle,' says John B. 'We hoped that would give us the key to get in. And in case anyone is wondering why we called it the Double Dubb, we gave it that name because in America we call Volkswagens V Dubs.'

The team acquired one of the Volkswagens before they even knew their application had been accepted, and used their network of vintage car enthusiasts in the San Francisco and Palo Alto area to get components for the best prices possible. Despite this, John S estimates that they ended up spending around £4000 building the car. He points out, however, that they plan to be back on budget soon. 'That needs some

'From the very beginning the idea was to sell them a strange vehicle. We hoped that would give us the key to get in'

explaining doesn't it?' he smiles. 'The biggest single item that we bought was the pump for the hydraulic steering. That came to eight or nine hundred dollars. Half way through we needed some advice so we called the manufacturer. We told the guy what we were doing and he said, "If I had known that I would have given you a pump," so he gave us a spare one.'

'I don't think we're going to need it now,' says Jay, 'so we're planning to sell it when we get home. That should put us back on budget.'

Double Dubb was built at the workshop John B uses to restore vintage cars. 'I would do my regular work and then try to switch over at about four o'clock,' he says, 'but in the end I pretty much worked on our car all the time.' John B was joined by John S and Jay, and the team claim that they didn't take a single day off during the build period.

The result of their labours is stylish and innovative, but unusually light compared to many of the other vehicles in the competition. 'I'm not worried about that,' says Jay. 'We have a strong, safe machine – the cage and the welding are both first rate. Obviously we don't want any collisions, but if anything tries to muscle in then we'll just back out. We've got a top speed of 60 kph, although I don't think we'll ever get to use that here. One thing we know is that the producers aren't going to let anyone get hurt.

'We haven't set out to build the ultimate fighting machine,' Jay continues. 'We're prepared for contest, not battle. We set out to build something that was kind of off-the-wall, and to make it as good as we possibly could. If I had to advise anyone how to get on in this show, I'd tell them to read the rules carefully: be prepared for contest rather than battle. A lot of vehicles seem to have been made for jousting, and we don't think that's what this is going to be about. From what little we've seen, the courses seem to have the feel of carnival games.

'The only other advice I'd offer is choose your team-mates well. There are people here who've never worked with each other before, and I can't imagine what that must have been like. I feel I've really got to know my father doing this, because I left home a while ago and this has given us the chance to work closely together. It's been a great experience for all of us.'

CALIFORNIA
HOT RODS

Diary Extracts

Day 4
Checked our expenditure. Ouch - now at $2700!

Day 8
Fitted upper frame and main structure. Now the form and shape evolves.

Day 9
The chassis looks very 'boxy'. Hung both engines on and the shape changed. Took advice from Dave Willis and now have a good direction to achieve a shapely vehicle.

Day 10
Batteries, gas tank, throttle, firewalls - done!

Day 12
Mother's Day - but made good progress. Upper pivot in place - now a true articulator.

Day 13
John B has it all tacked together but there are hours and hours of welding to go before it is whole.

Day 18
It runs! It's OK! Front engine still needs tuning but in all its fundamental features the DD meets or exceeds our expectations. It is powerful and really manoeuvrable.

Day 23
Finalise systems for off-road test. New carbs great improvement but still need more work.

Day 30
Final paint touch-up by Dave Willis - and it's over!

Double Dubb

DONOR VEHICLE
Two Volkswagen Bugs

ENGINE TYPE
Two VW 1600cc

TRANSMISSION TYPE
Manual

ESTIMATED WEIGHT
1600 kg

OVERALL LENGTH
12 feet 6 inches

WIDTH
5 feet

HEIGHT
6 feet

SUSPENSION TYPE
VW torsian bar

FUEL TYPE
Petrol

OTHER FEATURES
Four-wheel drive. Articulated hydraulic steering

'We're prepared for contest, not battle'

The Ice Vikings
Reykjavik, Iceland

Rafn Hardarson

Team captain Rafn is a member of the same motor sports club as Sverrir and Haldor. Rafn races and builds cars for Formula 1 and off-roading and has used his excellent welding skills in the construction of the team's vehicle. He has the following message for the other teams: 'We are going to eat you!'

Sverrir Ingjaldsson

Sverrir is from a family of car mechanics and built his first vehicle – a three-wheeled go-kart – at the age of 13. He recalls riding it to school before it was seized by the police. Sverrir is extremely confident about his team's chances in *Full Metal Challenge*. 'I think we're going to win,' he says in a matter-of-fact way. 'We're good.'

Haldor Bjornsson

Haldor's devotion to his hobby seems to have come at the expense of his love life. 'I don't think any girl would put up with the life I'm living,' he says. 'All my time and money is spent on motorsports.' Haldor is 27, and the youngest member of the team, but he has already competed in over 70 races.

As probably befits the team from Reykjavik, the Ice Vikings are a cool bunch. The language barrier only seems to add to the team's apparently impassive demeanour, and they frustratingly refuse to melt during our brief conversation.

'We heard about *Full Metal Challenge* when we came across it on the internet,' says Sverrir. 'It looked interesting so we decided to give it a try. We all collaborated on a design and it was accepted quite quickly without any problems.'

The result was Thor, a dragster-style vehicle that was constructed in a workshop belonging to one of their friends. 'We got the shell from one old car and the chassis and engine from another,' says Rafn. The chassis and V8 engine came from a Ford, which became the basis for the rugged four-wheel drive vehicle.

Thor boasts good traction for rough and steep terrains and a reasonable 250 horsepower for speed and acceleration but is slightly compromised by its turning circle; its manoeuvrability might not be as good as that of other vehicles in the competition.

The team admit to having gone slightly over budget, and seem sincere when they say that the 30-day deadline to complete the vehicle posed little or no problem. Despite that, Haldor concedes that they only managed to find 30 minutes to test the vehicle before it was shipped off to England. They ran Thor up and down some hills above a disused mine and caused some damage in the process. 'We didn't have too many problems,' says Haldor, 'but when we tested it we broke a few things. After the testing we had to fix the front suspension to make it a little bit stronger, but we learned enough to enable us to add a few extra things as well.'

On their tinkering day at the *Full Metal Challenge* site, the team took Thor out for three brief test runs and returned confident enough to declare that the vehicle was 'strong enough' for the rigours of the courses ahead. Resplendent in its blue, white and red paint job – the colours of the

'You almost wet your pants but you do it again!'

Iceland flag – Thor stood out amongst many of its squat and lumbering counterparts on the strength of its looks alone. 'We're not worried about the courses,' says Rafn, 'and we're not worried about reliability. Thor only weighs 1650 kilograms – we're far more worried about contact with other vehicles while we're out there.'

All three team-members are sharing the driving, and as all three are qualified and equally passionate there are expected to be some heated debates about who gets behind the wheel on the first day of filming. One thing the team are agreed on is that the best features of their car are its speed capabilities and its suspension. 'I love speed,' says Haldor. 'It's a fantastic feeling; you almost wet your pants but you do it again!'

Sverrir is rather more down-to-earth when analysing the appeal of the team's vehicle. 'We won't stand much impact,' he says. 'We need to be fast.'

'I think we're going to win. We're good'

Thor

DONOR VEHICLE
Ford F250

ENGINE TYPE
Ford 5.8L

TRANSMISSION TYPE
Manual

ESTIMATED WEIGHT
1650 kg

OVERALL LENGTH
4 feet 8 inches

WIDTH
7 feet

HEIGHT
6 feet 8 inches

SUSPENSION TYPE
Leaf spring

FUEL TYPE
Petrol

OTHER FEATURES
Four-wheel drive

Rollercoaster

Aim of the game: complete the course as quickly as possible

Rollercoaster is probably the most intricate and visually impressive course on the Full Metal Challenge site. The course resembles a giant version of the board game Mousetrap, and forces the drivers to maintain precise control over their vehicles at all times.

This aptly named game has the look and feel of a fairground rollercoaster ride on raised tracks. It contains wedge and high-pivot 50 feet teeters, obstacles and tipping bumps designed to destabilise a passing vehicle. The game also features a 30 degree inverse camber bend. Cameras watch from the sides and above as each driver attempts to negotiate this precarious course in the fastest time possible. This is a test of speed, traction and manoeuvrability.

The Rules

Teams will attempt the course one at a time and will have one attempt each. Teams must stay on the track. If a vehicle comes off the track it must get back on at the same point to complete the course. It will incur a ten second time penalty each time it leaves the track.

Indian Hope Trick
Delhi, India

Raj Kapoor
Team captain Raj won his first rally competition in 1984 and established his own auto business in 1990. 'Cars play a major role in my life,' he says. 'I like to read about them, talk about them and drive them.' He admits that his wife regards him as a lost cause.

Jayesh Desai
Jayesh started his own auto business in 1989, and has been a keen rally driver for even longer. He especially enjoys rally-driving in the Himalayas due to the extremes of temperature and impressive landscapes. Together with his team-mates he is a co-organiser of the annual Raid de Himalaya rally.

Vijay Parmar
Vijay was a champion motorcyclist in the 1980s and 90s and is just as enthusiastic about cars as he is bikes. He owns his own auto business in Shimla area, and devotes much of his spare time to his duties as president of the Himalayan Motorsport Association.

Morale is low in the Indian team, and it's not surprising. They had probably the most traumatic build time of any team in the competition – war was looming with Pakistan, disrupting the visa applications of the RDF camera crew hoping to film their progress. Following a breakdown in communication, Indian Hope Trick were left wondering whether they were even still a part of the show. Happily, those misunderstandings were resolved – in time for the team to discover that they had a week less than they thought to complete their machine as its passage to England had already been booked. A mix-up with the shipping company responsible for taking their car to England only added to the headaches; in the end the vehicle was air-freighted.

Luckily, all three men are level-headed professionals, so were able to triumph over adversity. They have been friends since college, and are now co-organisers of India's biggest motor sport event, the Raid de Himalaya. Team captain Raj takes his hobby, and his participation in the sport, very seriously indeed, but his intensity is partly offset by the bubbly, light-hearted nature of his team-mate Vijay. The mood among all three men lightens when they discuss the inspiration for the name of their vehicle.

'It's called Delhi Belly,' says Vijay with a knowing smile. It's clear that the name isn't only a reference to the car's egg-shaped design. 'Anyone who has ever visited India will know what Delhi Belly means.'

Jayesh adds: 'Just like the medical condition, we hope our car will cause an upset!'

The design of Delhi Belly was a joint effort, but the hardest part of the process was finding components to construct it. The team stress that the huge cultural difference between India and the Western countries in the competition made it harder for them to compete on a level footing. 'In this country there is a disposable mentality,' says Jayesh. 'When something has been used it is thrown away.'

'Anyone who has ever visited India will know what Delhi Belly means'

He illustrates the point by holding aloft a plastic cup he has plucked from a water dispenser. 'You would drink from this cup and then put it in the bin. That mentality doesn't exist in India: things are used and recycled until they simply no longer function, so it was virtually impossible for us to find useful discarded components. In India, junkyards contain just that - junk. We went over budget because a lot of the parts we needed we had to order new, often from places like Australia. It was very expensive - we ended up spending an amount equal to that which RDF had given us.'

Raj explains that they were able to source a few components from other vehicles: 'We took the chassis from a Suzuki jeep and the engine from a Vauxhall Ambassador. There are lots of other bits and pieces - some spare parts from a Mini Cooper, the wheels from an Allegro and so on.

'We had to keep the weight of the vehicle down because the engine is quite small,' continues Raj. 'If another vehicle bears down on us we'll have to run like hell. Other than that I won't know how well prepared we are until I see the courses. I haven't even had time to drive the vehicle until now.'

'Having seen the other vehicles I think we would have strengthened the sides of our car if we had the chance,' says Vijay, 'but our car is narrow and I think it will shift across rather than crash if there is a side impact. The radiator is in the driver's cabin so we have to do everything we can to avoid a front collision. If anything does happen, we're hoping it will be relatively easy to make a recovery because we're so light.'

'In India they have hardly ever seen anyone try something like this,' says Jayesh. 'We're very pleased to be here for that reason, but the best part of this event is that people have had the chance to use their inspiration and come up with their own designs.' Raj agrees: 'Some people have incredible imaginations and have put together some crazy things.'

'The quality of all the people competing is excellent,' says Vijay. 'The quality of the work is clear, but so is the level of insane genius!'

Delhi Belly

DONOR VEHICLE
Suzuki Jeep
Vauxhall Ambassador
Isuzu Trooper

ENGINE TYPE
Four cylinder inline
80 bhp

TRANSMISSION TYPE
Manual

ESTIMATED WEIGHT
1200 kg

OVERALL LENGTH
12 feet

WIDTH
5 feet 6 inches

HEIGHT
6 feet

SUSPENSION TYPE
Leaf spring with twin shocks all around

FUEL TYPE
Petrol

OTHER FEATURES
Four-wheel drive

Raid de Himalaya

Raj, Jayesh and Vijay are among the organisers of the Raid de Himalaya, the most arduous - and certainly the highest - motoring event in India. The event was established in 1999, and covers approximately 2600 kilometres, over a thousand of which are traversed under competitive conditions. The competitive stretch includes the freezing desert conditions from Gramphoo to Kaza, where the temperature can plunge to minus 20 degrees. The highest part of the course is the Tanglang-La Pass, which reaches an oxygen-starved altitude of 17,584 feet. The fourth Raid de Himalaya was held in October 2002, and introduced some changes to the course and duration. Raj, Jayesh, Vijay and the other organisers decided to make the course a little less arduous and reduced the duration to four days in order to put the emphasis back on adventure rather than endurance.

The Kalahari Cats
Cape Town, South Africa

Mike Rideout
Team captain Mike turned his hobby of fixing 4x4s into a career, and continues to pursue such extra-curricular interests as racing Land Rovers off-road. He owns a 4x4 outfitters and a yard that repairs safari expedition cars. He is confident that his team's skills and considerable experience will pay dividends.

Guy Fielding
47-year-old Guy hails from London but has been in South Africa for 26 years. He doesn't seem terribly sentimental about England and bemoans the fact that South Africans are 'ignored down here at the bottom of the world.' Winning *Full Metal Challenge* would, of course, help to change all that....

Gavin Coatcee
Gavin is just 21 years old and is leaving South Africa for the first time in order to discover whether his ace welding has paid off. Gavin is shy and quiet, but reveals that he supports Liverpool and that he's excited to be visiting Britain.

The Kalahari Cats have come a long way to take part in *Full Metal Challenge* and are raring to go. Guy Fielding cannot wait 'to show the Yanks and Brits a thing or two' and his friend Mike is getting frustrated: 'There's too much sitting around,' he grumbles. 'We just want to get in there. The whole thing's dragging on.' The third member of the team, 20-year-old Gavin Coatcee, maintains a respectful silence in the presence of his older team-mates, satisfied that he's already surmounted the major personal hurdle of getting on a plane. 'I was more nervous about flying than taking part in this competition,' he smiles, revealing the missing teeth which he lost in the days when he was a gang-member. It would seem that Mike and Guy didn't offer their nervous young friend much support. 'We gave him a hard time over the flying thing,' says Mike, laughing. Guy seems equally amused by Gavin's anxiety. 'He was so frightened on the way over I thought he was going to sit on my lap!'

The South African team were relative latecomers in the application process. By the time they found out about the competition from a friend in the United States there were only two days left in which to submit a formal application. 'I stayed up late and did some designs for a vehicle,' says Guy, 'and RDF liked them. I'm very glad that the vehicle has stayed true to those basic designs.'

'I'm going to be honest here and say that I think we got accepted not because of our design but because we were a South African team,' says Mike. 'We're the only team from anywhere in Africa. There are people from Australia, Russia and South America, but we're the only team from South Africa and I think they thought that would look great on the show. Our vehicle is based on a Range Rover, and since I've arrived here I've discovered that there a lot of other Range Rovers and Land Rovers taking part. If we could audition all over again I would have suggested a different design for our car, not because I think there's anything wrong with it but because there are so

'If we could audition all over again I would have suggested a different design for our car'

'We're impatient to get out there, but really we're just here for the fun of it'

many other Range Rovers around here.'

The team spent half their budget acquiring a V8 Range Rover which had won a number of competitions but which the team admit had been reduced to the status of 'a wreck'. They set to work by shortening the chassis and adding a roll cage and a defensive aluminium tread plate. A pneumatically operated differential lock was added to the front differential, with the aim of improving the traction on rough terrains. Throughout the whole process Guy and Mike employed Gavin's excellent welding and mechanical skills. The car was built in Mike's business's workshop, and by the last week time was getting so tight that he was turning customers away in order to devote time and space to completing the vehicle on schedule. Thirty days and 30,000 rand later, the result was a basic but efficient machine which they christened the Leopard.

'It's a bit of a plain Jane but I'm not worried about that,' says Guy. 'I've spent quite a while in the workshop talking to some of the other teams. Some of them have come up with very elaborate vehicles, and now they're pacing up and down because they're worried they won't work on the day. We don't have that worry.'

Mike nods in agreement. 'A lot of guys have decided to floor it on the test-drive and have come back to the workshop with things damaged. Some of them have literally taken off out there and now need repairing. When we did our test drive we just checked that the steering was OK before we came back and put it away. We don't have excessive features and controls to worry about, and we're comfortable with that.'

'There are a lot of nervous people out there, and a lot of people who are really out to win,' says Mike. 'We're impatient to get out there, but really we're just here for the fun of it.'

Leopard

DONOR VEHICLE
Range Rover

ENGINE TYPE
V8 3.5

TRANSMISSION TYPE
Manual

ESTIMATED WEIGHT
2400 kilograms

OVERALL LENGTH
10 feet

WIDTH
5 feet

HEIGHT
6 feet

SUSPENSION TYPE
Coil

FUEL TYPE
Petrol

OTHER FEATURES
Four-wheel drive

Kiwi Thunder
Auckland, New Zealand

Trevor McCoid

Team captain Trevor spent 20 years in the Royal New Zealand Navy but now owns Albany Mowers, NZ's largest lawnmower store. He estimates that his company caters for around a third of the population's grass disposal needs. His advice to anyone intending to follow in his team's footsteps is simple: 'Open your eyes.'

Kent McCoid

Kent is Trevor's son, and living proof that motor vehicles are in the family's blood. Kent got his driving licence aged 15 and completed an auto apprenticeship before he started working at Albany as a car engineer and sales manager. His welding skills came in useful during the build. Kent will be sharing the driving with his cousin, Steve.

Steve McCoid

Steve is Trevor's nephew, and makes up the strong and silent element of the team. Steve is a highly qualified technician who is currently adding to his knowledge by studying electrical engineering. He has travelled extensively, spending ten years in Australia. He plans to return there, and aims to ride around the country by motorbike.

Full Metal Challenge is a competition largely contested between big vehicles with big, roaring engines. For so many of the drivers and their attendant mechanics and engineers, the philosophy is very clearly 'the bigger the better' and one gets the impression that some teams intend to subjugate the course and their opponents by simply flattening everything in their path. Given this overbearing atmosphere, it is surprising to meet a family team who are pinning their hopes on a vehicle that is based on a sit-down lawnmower.

There is method to the apparent madness of New Zealand's Kiwi Thunder team, who embarked on their mechanical journey with the commendable goal of constructing a vehicle from scratch. 'We wanted to get into what we saw as the true spirit of the show,' says Kent. 'We also thought that by building from scratch we'd ultimately be able to do more with our vehicle. Those weren't the only reasons for not using a donor vehicle – we didn't want the hassle of buying an old machine and then worrying about whether it was going to be reliable or not.'

Before they knew they'd been accepted to take part in the show, the team contacted the Auckland University of Technology to see if any of the academics there were interested in finding a practical outlet for their computer-modelling skills. They eventually met David White, a senior lecturer at the university's Faculty of Science and Engineering. 'I invited David, a hydraulic engineer and a fabrication engineer to come along to a meeting,' says Trevor. 'I asked them all to draw what they thought we should build. They all presented me with designs for four-wheel drive vehicles, and I wasn't very surprised. I then said to them, "Watch this," and I got Kent to jump onto one of the mowers. He started it up and demonstrated its manoeuvrability while they watched. I said, "Guess what guys – that's what we're going to build!" You should have seen their faces. To us it seemed like the natural way to go, because

'We wanted to deliver exactly what we'd promised'

lawnmowers are our business and we're mechanics, not design engineers.'

Once he'd recovered from the shock, Professor White stayed on to provide computer-animated 3D models from the team's design in an effort to reassure RDF that the vehicle would be suitably robust. Having decided to take the difficult – and most expensive – route to creating a vehicle, the team had to find the time and the money they needed. The team's car, the Black Thunder, may be based on a lawnmower but that's where the similarities largely end. The vehicle has a diesel engine with hydraulic motors. Independent wheel-steering and braking give it excellent traction and a remarkable zero-turn circle that is unrivalled by any other machine in the competition.

'We designed a hydraulic vehicle,' says Trevor, 'but to buy the hydraulics that we originally wanted would have cost us around $14,000 – these things are much more expensive in New Zealand than they are in the United States. We ended up buying the biggest hydraulics we could get off the shelf, and we were therefore restricted by what was available. We could have had what we wanted shipped from America and we would have paid less but that would have taken six weeks and we just didn't have the time.'

Black Thunder was constructed in the workshops at Albany Mowers, and the team struggled to get as much work done as possible without compromising the business. 'We did our normal work, delivering lawnmowers and demonstrating them during the day,' says Kent. 'Obviously we couldn't tell customers to go away because we wanted to get on with building our vehicle! We would work on the vehicle in the evenings. It was winter in New Zealand, however, and the weather was getting worse all the time. It got wetter and wetter and the days got shorter and shorter. By the time we'd finished the days were getting dark at 5.00 pm.'

'We didn't have a lot of time to test it but we did find a lot of problems,' says Steve. 'At first we put boat controls on it thinking they would make things easier but they made it too difficult to drive, and the hydraulics were just too high for it. The testing we did was quite aggressive – we tried to roll it to make sure it was safe and sound under extreme conditions. We're not worried about the engine or the brakes now – mechanically it's OK.'

'We could have changed the design to make it easier for us,' says Trevor. 'For example, if we had told RDF that we actually wanted to make a four-wheel drive vehicle instead I'm sure they would have accepted that. But we didn't want to do that,' he stresses, emphasising every word to illustrate his determination. 'We wanted to deliver exactly what we promised.'

'We've got something that the other teams haven't got,' says Steve, 'and that's something we call Kiwi ingenuity. This doesn't always manifest itself in radical ways, but it enables you to think outside the square to find different ways to create or modify something.'

'You can't define Kiwi ingenuity really,' says Kent. 'It's a state of mind that was shared by all of us, including all the people who helped us out and donated components. No one tried to change our minds – they all helped to make it work for us.'

'Kiwi ingenuity is a feeling,' says Trevor. 'It's a way of life.'

Black Thunder

DONOR VEHICLE
None

ENGINE TYPE
2 litre
80 bhp

TRANSMISSION TYPE
None

ESTIMATED WEIGHT
1300 kilograms

OVERALL LENGTH
6 feet 8 inches

WIDTH
4 feet 8 inches

HEIGHT
4 feet 4 inches

SUSPENSION TYPE
None

FUEL TYPE
Diesel

OTHER FEATURES
Hydraulic two-wheel drive
with castor front wheels

Wetropolis
Aim of the game: complete the course, driving round obstacles in reverse, as quickly as possible

Wetropolis takes place on a surreal waterlogged pitch that contains three giant fire hydrants. A vehicle can only complete the course once it has made a 360 degree loop around each fire hydrant before returning to the finishing line.

Each team must race one at a time through the water. The complete loop around each fire hydrant must be made in reverse. The fastest team wins.

Cameras suspended on retractable hydraulic arms monitor the progress of the vehicles from every angle. This test of speed and manoeuvrability will push many of the drivers and their machines to the limit as they become submerged in deep water.

The Rules

Drivers must tackle the entire hydrant-looping part of the course with their vehicle in reverse.
Each team is only allowed one attempt.
The order and direction in which they circle the hydrants is up to each driver.
The fastest vehicle to complete the course wins.

POLICE

THE LAW DAWGS

The Law Dawgs
California, USA

Tom Rea
Team captain Tom has been a policeman for 17 years, and although he is the most senior Law Dawg in every respect he is generous with his praise of his colleagues: 'Dave and Mike have amazed me multiple times with their ingenuity,' he says. Tom's hobbies include racing go-karts and motorbikes.

Dave Corder
Like Tom, Dave is leaving the United States for the first time to take part in *Full Metal Challenge*. Dave is the most mischievous, light-hearted member of the team, whose expert driving and welding skills have been an asset. During the course of his duties, Dave can drive for 11 hours a day, sometimes reaching speeds of 120 mph.

Mike Hicks
Mike was a Police Academy driving champion, and has been involved in well over a hundred high-speed pursuits. He builds hot rods as a hobby, and is well qualified to be the team's principal driver. 'We don't care what country they're from,' he says of his *FMC* rivals, 'we want to kick their butt!'

The town of Modesto nestles in California's sunny Stanislaus County. Modesto's major claim to fame is as the birthplace of *Star Wars* creator George Lucas, who has never strayed far (Skywalker Ranch, the headquarters of the Lucasfilm organisation, is situated nearby). George Lucas came to prominence not with *Star Wars*, but with the 1973 movie *American Graffiti*, which kick-started the 1950s nostalgia boom and eulogised the dragster-racing days of Lucas's youth. The film was shot entirely on location in and around the nearby San Rafael.

 'I guess the area's famous for *American Graffiti*,' says team captain Tom, 'and hot rods!' Tom, Dave and Mike dispute my perception of Modesto as a sleepy backwater, claiming that the town has a crime problem just like any other. 'It's not that bad,' says Mike, 'but unfortunately things like murder, robbery and rape do occur. We have to deal with several robberies a month – in fact we had one the week before we flew out here.'

 'There was a high-speed chase,' adds Tom. 'We chased him for ten minutes. The longest chase we had was 33 minutes. It went on for about 35 miles and then my car blew up – I got in another one and carried on. The guy's in prison now.'

 'I've been in car chases with Mike, and I think he's a great driver,' says Dave. 'That's why he's the main driver for this competition.'

 Other than having to drive under arduous conditions, the team say that their professional experience has prepared them for the *Full Metal Challenge* experience in other ways. 'We're trained to deal with pressurised situations,' says Tom. 'We have stay level and cool when we're on duty, and we had to stay level and cool when we were working to the deadline building the vehicle.'

 Although two members of the team are former police dog handlers, The Law Dawgs got their name when they competed in *Junkyard Wars*. They resisted the production team's suggestion that they call themselves The Deputy Dawgs and arrived at mutually acceptable compromise.

'We don't care what country they're from, we want to kick their butt!'

The Law Dawgs' vehicle Impact Weapon may not be the heaviest car in the competition but its size and imposing design are enough to dominate the *FMC* workshop. The name was another element drawn from the team's police experience. 'The term "impact weapon" is used by police in the States to describe a retractable baton, or, as you'd call it in the UK, a truncheon,' explains Dave. 'Sometimes you need to use a level of force to deal with a suspect on arrest.'

When not tinkering with Impact Weapon, Tom, Dave and Mike wandered around the workshop, checking out the competition. 'We spent some time with our own vehicle, looking for weak spots,' says Dave. 'We spent three or four days testing it, and that taught us a lot. We discovered that our braking system [the two front wheels have hydraulic brakes] didn't work the way we planned it, so we re-fabricated it. We've been looking at the other vehicles since we got here, trying to see their potential weaknesses.'

'When we designed the vehicle, we decided as our starting point to keep the framework light,' says Mike. 'We also knew we wanted it to be four-wheel drive. We had a list of priorities, but we also had to be flexible; when some of the parts we wanted didn't come through we had to adapt our design.'

The team spent a total of $3428 on parts and materials to build the car. 'We had to be very careful about how we used the money,' says Tom. 'Over half the parts were things that we had just lying around. To build a quality machine is expensive. It's like, "How fast do we want it to go?" and the answer is, "How much money have we got?"'

Building a *Full Metal Challenge* vehicle has been a huge commitment for all the teams, and the support and understanding of family-members is crucial. 'When we first told our wives I don't think they thought we'd be building the car for that long,' says Dave. 'My wife was relieved that we were building the car at our house, but I think she was surprised that we spent so long in the workshop. All she saw of me of four weeks were glimpses through the kitchen window. And she's got so used to seeing Mike that she now calls him her brother. On some days we worked on the vehicle for 14 hours. I'm lucky I have understanding neighbours!'

'It's like, "How fast do we want it to go?" and the answer is, "How much money have we got?"'

POLICE

Diary Extracts

Day 1
Pulled the engine, transmission and transfer case out of the Blazer. Also removed the drivelines.

Day 2
Pulled axles out of Blazer, attached springs and fitted them under frame. By end of today we had a rolling chassis.

Day 5
Spent most of evening after work on assembly of engine – mounting heads, intake manifold and HEI ignition system.

Day 8
Installed engine and drive train in frame.

Day 10
Had to fabricate opposite side radiator outlets (ugh!). Worked on gas lines and mounted fuel cell. At midnight we fired up engine. It sounded great, but got hot quickly. Cooling system needs major work. Mike punctured fuel cell while cutting inspection door. Ouch!

Day 12
We road-tested the split front brake system on the dirt-road behind Dave's house. Wow! Cut the wheel, stomp the left brake, stab the throttle and the car will make a U-turn in 24 feet! Very encouraging.

Day 14
Installed the transfer case conversion so we have the option to use two-wheel drive.

Day 22
Finished body panels and completed most of bodywork.

Day 26
Took car to local ranch via trailer and did some testing. Engine and gears work great! Engine runs a little warm, starter had problems when it heated up. Also problem with front springs.

Day 29
Today was the day to drive all over creation and pick up parts. The drive line (front) was finished and I [Tom] picked it up from the shop I used to work at. When I explained what we were doing the roll bar padding was also donated!

'We struggled with the money and the time'

because we were already committed to getting so much of our own work done. We had to use the weekends to get it finished. At least we were able to use the BAS workshop and all its facilities to build the vehicle. I've been talking to some of the other guys here, and some of them have told me that they built their cars at home. I don't know how they did it, although I must say that some of the engineering I've seen here has been fantastic. The hydraulics on some of those cars must have blown the budgets by themselves.'

'We knew we couldn't go too much over budget, because we didn't have a lot of our own money to put into it,' says Chris. 'To be honest, the only reason we went slightly over was because when we were testing we broke a spring. The camera crew came to film us on the last day, and after we'd finished off a few things we started testing it. We didn't push the vehicle too far, but it is very old and we really should have stopped and checked it over but we carried on. We knew it was going to rain, and the camera crew were filming, so we kept going and going and going. Then we went over some rough terrain and broke one of the springs.'

Rod and Dave are married, while Chris describes himself as 'young, free and single'. The building schedule placed a particular strain on Dave's private life. 'I just married last year [2001],' he says, 'and after I got married I went off to the Antarctic for six months so it wasn't very fair on Sarah, my wife. She was a little bit pissed off at the time of the build because it occurred at the same time as our wedding anniversary and her birthday. It didn't go down very well, me leaving the house at 7.00 am and coming home at 9.00 at night.'

Now the traumatic building and testing periods are behind them, The Pole Cats are facing the trials of actually competing. 'I know we're carrying a lot of weight,' says Dave, 'but I'm not too worried about that. We have big military wheels, which are quite tough, so I think we'll be able to cope with collisions. We don't know what the courses consist of, but I'm sure they've been designed to cope with different types of vehicles, and I'm sure that different types of vehicles will do well in different types of events.'

When asked whether the team-members have any advise for anyone considering competing in *Full Metal Challenge* Rod answers. 'My advice?' he says, laughing. 'Have more than £2000!'

White Noise

DONOR VEHICLE
Tucker Sno-Cat
Bedford military truck
(axles and wheels)

ENGINE TYPE
Cummins V6 turbo
170 bhp

TRANSMISSION TYPE
Automatic

ESTIMATED WEIGHT
3060 kilograms

WIDTH
7 feet 10 inches

SUSPENSION TYPE
Leaf spring

FUEL TYPE
Diesel

OTHER FEATURES
Four-wheel drive

Ravine deep, mountain high

The Sno-Cat oversnow vehicle is a four-tracked workhorse that has been manufactured by the Tucker Sno-Cat Corroboration for over 60 years. The company's slogan is 'No Snow Too Deep... No Road Too Deep' and this would seem to be true, for the Sno-Cat and its various spin-offs (such as the Sno-Kitten) have become the most highly respected and enduring vehicles of their type.

The classic four-tracked design which still prevails was introduced in 1951. Each of the four tracks is independently sprung and pivoted at the drive axle. At first glance the vehicle's cab might seem conventional, but under the bonnet the vehicle is customised to cope with rough and steep terrain and is highly adaptable. Sno-Cats are hydraulically steered by pivoting both axles, and their engines can be situated to the rear or the centre – the four-track arrangement ensures that the vehicle's distribution of weight remains good. Sno-Cats were used in the first motorised crossing of Antarctica in 1957 and are still driven by research teams based in the area. Tucker continue to manufacture between 60 and 70 new Sno-Cats every year.

King of the Hill
Aim of the game: be the first to conquer the king hill in the centre of the course

King of the Hill is a game of territorial conquest. The game takes place on a pitch comprising six small hills which surround a larger central hill. Teams must conquer two of the smaller hills by hitting a post at the top of the hill, before attempting to conquer the central king hill. All three teams are together on the pitch, competing to get to the top and conquer the smaller hills before each other.
Cameras watch this test of agility and traction from the sides and from above.

The Rules

Teams must conquer two of the smaller hills before they make an attempt on the larger central hill. There are only certain hills that the teams are allowed to attempt – one which is solely theirs, and two others which they and one other team can attempt.

To conquer a hill, the teams must hit a central post at the top of the hill sufficiently hard to cause an explosion to go off.

In the event of two teams competing on the same hill, referees will judge which team actually hit the post. Vehicles must not leave the safety area around the perimeter of the course.

The Russian Bears

Moscow, Russia

Team captain Max is a lecturer at Moscow State University, where he instructs students on such complex subjects as the function of drive trains on tanks. He has good welding skills and his hobbies include 'anything to do with engines'. He describes his cousins Evgueni and Alexey as his 'right and left hands.'

Evgueni is the deputy manager of an engineering firm, but outside work hours he has gained considerable driving experience. He is an award-winning rally driver and his hobbies include working alongside his team-mates fixing cars. He seems overjoyed at the prospect of pursing this leisure activity on a bigger scale for *Full Metal Challenge*.

29-year-old Alexey is Evgueni's younger brother and the most junior member of the team. He jokes that Max and Evgueni waited for him to be born in order to give him the most unpleasant jobs. Alexey is a mechanic at the same engineering firm where Evgueni works. He has excellent engine and transmission skills, and is also a specialist in metalwork.

First impressions of The Russian Bears suggest that the team will live up to their name. These burly Muscovites seem a cold and unfriendly bunch, and as neither Evgueni nor Alexey speak any English they seem especially remote. Through the efforts of an interpreter and the English-speaking Max we soon find some common ground and the bears turn out to be pussy cats. The *Beavis and Butt-head*-style nervous giggling of Evgueni and Alexey is infectious, and before long all three team-mates are convulsed in fits on uncontrollable laughter. In fact the slightest thing seems to set this lot off, and they turn out to be perhaps the most frivolous of all the teams in the competition.

'Let's face it,' says Max. 'Having only 30 days to build is not so bad when you consider that last year [2001] Evgueni and I went to California to take part in a *Junk/Scrap* special called *Megawars*. On that occasion we had only two days to make something out of bits we scavenged from a pile of junk, so in some ways having a month felt like a bit of luxury!' Cue more laughter.

Max, Evgueni and Alexey were invited to take part in *Full Metal Challenge* following the aforementioned jaunt to California, and set about designing a vehicle based on a military truck. The dubbed their design Siberian Monster. 'The "Monster" part is easy to explain,' says Max. 'It was called "Monster" simply because it was so huge. The "Siberian" part came from the diesel engine that we were going to use – it was taken from a vehicle that had spent 20 years working in Siberia. However, when we got the engine we realised that if we used it we would have gone well over the weight restrictions. Our estimate was that our original design would have weighed six-and-a-half tons. So we decided to come up with a different design, but by that time we'd already come up with the name Siberian Monster and we thought it was so good we decided to keep it, whatever we ultimately built. The name was just

"My wife was crazy about me doing this. Actually that's a lie..."

too good to lose.'

The team had such difficulty finding the parts they needed, they decided that rather than spending time customising a car, they would buy a vehicle and concentrate on stripping it down. They bought a four-ton military truck and, according to Evgueni, 'we made a lot of changes, all in an effort to make the vehicle simpler.'

Working around their regular jobs, the team-mates convened at the worskhops of Evgueni's employer - the curiously un-Russian sounding O'Hara CIS Engineering. The company specialises in armour-plating vehicles for security services and diplomats, so was able to offer many of the tools the team needed, as well as the space.

'My wife was crazy about me doing this,' says Evgueni, describing the long hours in the workshop. He adds that Max and Alexey's girlfriends were similarly thrilled. 'Actually that's a lie,' he eventually admits, 'but they got used it. We even talked them into helping us - towards the end of the build the girls helped us paint the vehicle.'

The Siberian Monster was packed in a crate and shipped to England before the team got the opportunity to test drive it at all. A tentative 100 metre journey soon gave way to a more ambitious workout. During the team's second day behind the wheel the car briefly became airborne, and

fortunately survived the experience in one piece. 'We checked the ignition and made some slight modifications to the shift,' says Max. 'Nothing major.'

During their time in the workshop, the team have checked out the other vehicles and drawn comparisons with their own machine. 'Our vehicle is big and robust and strong,' says Evgueni, emitting a nervous laugh that possibly betrays the fact that for once he isn't as confident as he seems. 'The construction of our vehicle is quite simple compared to that of some of our rivals and I think this is an asset.'

'There are some weak points,' adds Alexey. 'I don't think it's protected enough from water, and I don't think the steering is powerful enough. We should be more manoeuvrable to take part in a competition like this, but the donor vehicle was not designed to be particularly agile - we are using steering that was designed for a truck.'

Team driver Evgueni does not yet know that games such as Hall of Mirrors and Rollercoaster will demand an agility that his vehicle may struggle to achieve, but he's aware that once filming begins he'll be out on his own without the morale-boosting bravado of his colleagues. And for once, the team seem to be agreed that that's no laughing matter.

'If you build a machine together, you all want to drive it together'

concealing the disdain in his voice. 'We followed the brief and entered into the spirit of the thing. There aren't many people here who did the same thing as us – literally made a machine from scratch.'

'I think it was much better to try to build a vehicle that way,' says Tariq, 'although I must admit that I don't think we knew what we were getting ourselves into when we started.'

'We had to be disciplined about it,' says Arie in his gruff, near impenetrable accent. 'We're always building things anyway so we had lots of bits in stock at George's workshop, which of course we were able to use as a build site. In these respects at least we were lucky.'

The Tartan Tinkerers called their vehicle Spartacus, and took its engine and chassis from a Leyland DAF Road Runner. One of its most striking aspects is its enormous size – the vehicle is a whopping 18 feet long and eight-and-a-half feet wide. It also features an unusual airbag at the front, to aid suspension; when the air bag fills, the front chassis lifts upwards.

The other most striking aspect of Spartacus is that it has six wheels. 'We did that because when we first got some information about the programme from RDF we decided to build a machine that could cope with extremely tough terrain. We added an extra axle at the back because we thought there might be boulders, pot-holes and so on out here. If there was a quarry here I think we would perform well. It's disappointing that there doesn't seem to be anything like that here.'

'I would say we built a machine that will cope fantastically well,' says Tariq, 'although there might be some events where it lets us down.'

'I think we'll do well in any events that involve water, heavy ground and big holes,' says George. 'I think our speed ability is on a par with most of the other vehicles I've seen here. Most of the people I've spoken to in the workshop seem to think they should have built a bigger machine actually. I'm not worried about that, and I'm not worried about collisions. Our vehicle wasn't built to withstand collisions, and we're not expecting a demolition derby. The only thing I'm nervous about really is the first event, whatever that may be. If we got out there and the machine collapsed straight away that would be terrible. Even if we lose our heat I want to have at least completed a full day.'

'Our vehicle's got good traction, but it's got weak points as well,' points out Arie. 'We did it the cheap way – if we'd done it in a more professional manner then it would have been more solid. I think six weeks or maybe two months would have been a more realistic deadline to build a better quality vehicle.'

Amongst Spartacus's potential weaknesses are the facts that the wheel axles are carrying a lot of strain and the drive chains look a little precarious – despite the team's confidence about rough terrain these could be prone to breaking on certain courses.

'We would like to win, but we have to be realistic,' Arie continues. 'I don't think we're going to win, so we're just going to go out there and enjoy it.'

Spartacus

DONOR VEHICLE
Leyland DAF Road Runner

ENGINE TYPE
6 cylinder (from above vehicle)

TRANSMISSION TYPE
Dry plate push type

ESTIMATED WEIGHT
3000 kilograms

OVERALL LENGTH
18 feet

WIDTH
8 feet 6 inches

HEIGHT
7 feet

SUSPENSION TYPE
Air/yoke

FUEL TYPE
Diesel

OTHER FEATURES
Four-wheel drive/six-wheel drive

Sumo
Aim of the game: disable the opposing vehicle or push it completely outside the ring

Like the ancient Oriental game, Sumo is played inside a circular arena. This arena, however, is 32 metres in diameter. Just like the real Sumo, the FMC version has two combatants – only this time round the wrestlers are monster vehicles.
A team can win either by pushing the opponent outside the ring, by disabling the opponent or if the other team surrenders. To make things even harder, the ring is zoned by different surfaces, many of them hazardous and slippy – some are filled with barbed wire and tyre spikes.
This is the last game in each round of the competition and is one of the games played inside the giant cooling towers. Cameras watch this test of brute force from the sides and from above.

The Rules

A disabled vehicle is one incapable of forward, backward or sideways movement under its own volition. A vehicle is deemed to be outside the ring if the entire body of the vehicle is beyond the perimeter – one or two wheels, or a track, is not sufficient. Linesmen will judge this. If there is no winner after two minutes then the ring will get smaller. If there is still no winner after another two minutes then the ring will get smaller still and the contest will continue until there is a winner. This is the only game in which the global rule concerning deliberately disabling another vehicle does not apply.

Three Shades of Grey
County Durham, United Kingdom

Peter Anderson

66-year-old Peter is captain of the most mature team in the competition, and proud of it. 'We have 150 years of experience between us and we are going to win!' he exclaims. Peter is a plant fitter and welder by trade, and his hobbies include sidecars, motocross, autograss, speedway and stock cars. He claims, 'There is nothing I have been asked to do that I couldn't do.'

Jim Anderson

At 68, agricultural engineer Jim is the oldest of the three Anderson brothers. Jim drives a Volvo estate he bought for £100. He customised the vehicle by installing a Daihatsu engine, a Ford Sierra gearbox and assorted bits from other cars, and claims the vehicle runs really well. His diverse hobbies include dancing, fell-running, stone-wall building and writing poetry.

Brian Anderson

Brian has been a mechanic for 50 years (since he was 15) and looked after Centurion tanks in the Middle East during the Suez Crisis. Nowadays he is a self-employed agricultural engineer and builds automata for theme pubs in his spare time. His other hobbies include restoring and racing motorbikes. Brian will be sharing the driving with Peter and Jim.

The vehicle created by the Three Shades of Grey team might resemble a small tank, but it is in fact a scratch-built creation featuring parts culled from a heavy goods vehicle, a farm tractor and a building site dumper. 'It's been a learning curve,' admits Jim. 'Building something from the floor up is near-impossible with the time and money allowed, but we don't have any regrets about doing it.'

'We've come out the other side of it now,' says Brian, casting his eyes towards the torrential downpour outside. 'Now that the hard work and stress is nearly over we've realised that it's brought us closer together.'

Three Shades of Grey are the only British team to have produced a vehicle with tracks. It wasn't until they started work that they decided on an appropriate name. 'There was so much to do,' remembers Brian, 'and every evening we would just collapse, exhausted. One evening, we finished work and were completely knackered when Peter started singing the old 1960s song "Wild Thing". We knew we had to call the vehicle something, and the title of the song just stuck.'

'It was a struggle to get it done on time,' concurs Jim, 'even though we had some help and we were working on it 12 hours a day. People will look at it say that it's impossible to build what we've made in 30 days, but we've proved them wrong. I'm not whinging about this, but some of the other vehicles here just look like a scout car with the top cut off.'

Wild Thing is indeed one of the most talked-about machines taking part in *Full Metal Challenge*, with many of the North American teams in particular stopping to admire the Anderson brothers' handiwork. 'I think it's the most innovative vehicle in the workshop,' boasts Brian. Peter adds: 'The workmanship is worth looking at. Whether we win or lose, I'm proud of what we've achieved just to build the machine and get as far as this.'

Wild Thing is clearly a solid piece of engineering,

'I think it's the most innovative vehicle in the workshop'

'We have 150 years of experience between us and we are going to win!'

and testament not only to the skills of the Andersons but also to their old-fashioned 'make do and mend' philosophy. One suspects that these gents feel a little alienated from today's throwaway culture and the modern reliance on computers.

'It's the best we could do in the time,' says Peter, philosophically. 'We were told there were going to be ten disciplines, so we built a vehicle that we hoped would do well in maybe seven of them. When we got here, however, we realised that there are only four disciplines in each particular heat. I think it's going to be a lottery which games we get to compete in first. We thought there was going to be a league, where you would compete in each of the ten events and the points you scored in each one would be accumulated. So we don't know which of the four games we'll get - I only hope that some consideration has been given to our vehicle's strengths.'

The Andersons have a few tricks up their sleeve, should the going get rough. The vehicle can contra-rotate - each track moving in an opposite direction from the other one - allowing it to spin round on its own axis. Other gizmos include the innovative hydro-pneumatic suspension which raises and lowers the vehicle allowing for a healthy ground clearance.

'We've got no conventional suspension, as such,' explains Brian. 'The arms which link the wheels are linked in turn to a hydraulic ram. We can lift and lower those arms at will, and consequently lift or lower the vehicle's ground clearance. You can't compress hydraulic oil, however, so within the hydraulic circuit we've got pressurised nitrogen spheres which give us a cushioned suspension effect.'

Hydraulic systems are notoriously expensive, and have been the financial bugbear of many teams in the competition. Three Shades of Grey were no exception. 'We spent £3000 in total,' says Peter, 'and a lot of that went on the hydraulics. We were initially concerned about the systems because we so busy building the vehicle that we only had about one hour to test it. Hydraulics aren't the kind of thing you can check just by looking at, and some of the stuff we got was second-hand so we were a bit concerned that we didn't have the time to test it properly. Since we arrived at the site, however, we've had a bit of time with the machine and nothing seems to be faulty.'

'Nothing's faulty,' agrees Brian, 'but a few things have been improved. Getting the opportunity to make improvements was very valuable. We still haven't had enough time to familiarise ourselves with the how the vehicle drives, but there's nothing we can do about that now. There's no point worrying - we just want to get on with it.'

A thunderstorm rumbles in the distance as the interview draws to a close. I wish the team luck, and express the hope that the weather improves for their first day of filming. 'Oh no,' says Brian, 'we'd prefer it if it rained all day. It will be much easier for us to manoeuvre if it's wet. We need to slip around a bit in order to turn. It can be as wet as it likes!'

Diary Extracts

Day 1
Panic sets in. Delivery of steel and enough box tube to part-assemble one side of the hull.

Day 6
Hull assembled – sheets cut for track guards and cut and bent for front and rear hull plates.

Day 10
Weld up link arm to pivots and spindles. Drill out wheel discs for weight-saving. Lathe work on wheel hubs. Assemble engine.

Day 16
More work on brakes – not an easy job. Sprockets assembled and welded up. Tracks fitted.

Day 18
Engine in and mounting finalised and fitted. Engine started up and running OK. Take engine out yet again, ready to fit hydraulic pump.

Day 25
Fill hydraulic tank, only to discover it has sprung a leak.

Day 26
Remove and re-weld hydraulic tank. Refit and refill (no leaks). Fit roll cage.

Day 28
Fit countershaft sprockets - yet more lathe work for Brian. Decide to fit pressure relief valves in motor drive pipelines.

Day 30
Decide to change drive ratios. Adjust control links and set relief valve pressures. See light at end of tunnel.

Day 31
Fit side-armour and engine stabiliser bars. Paint side-armour and go home. Early finish - 10.30 pm. Hooray!

Wild Thing

DONOR VEHICLE
None

ENGINE TYPE
Italian tractor engine, 60 bhp

TRANSMISSION TYPE
Hydraulic

ESTIMATED WEIGHT
2450 kg

OVERALL LENGTH
11 feet 6 inches

WIDTH
4 feet 6 inches

HEIGHT
5 feet 8 inches

SUSPENSION TYPE
Adjustable hydraulic

FUEL TYPE
Diesel

OTHER FEATURES
Tracks, and 'workmanship worth seeing!'

Tribal Force
Oklahoma, USA

Paul Shipman

Team captain Paul got a degree in engineering before joining the US Army to drive tanks. He later served in the National Guard. Eleven years after joining the army he returned to student life and gained a PhD in zoology. Paul is a member of the Cherokee tribe, and is very active in his local community. He makes drums, sings and plays at pow wows. Among his many talents he is also an expert in snake behaviour.

Edward Hara

'My brother and I are from a poor family,' says Edward, explaining how he gained his engineering skills. 'We got our education from The Better School of Roadside Mechanics: if the car broke down we had to fix it then and there!' During the preparations to compete in *Full Metal Challenge*, Edward completed his course in mechanical engineering at Oklahoma State University.

Leslie Hara

Leslie is an emergency room medical technician and the quietest member of Tribal Force. Les has worked as a farmhand, a truck driver and a welder, and spent six years in the electronics division of the US Navy. Like his brother Edward, Leslie is a member of the Ponca tribe. 'I guess you could say we're close relations to the Sioux,' he explains. Leslie's hobbies include rally cross driving and tinkering with cars.

Tribal Force seem shy and decidedly gentlemanly in comparison with some of the more forthright and aggressive competitors, and take their non-competitive stance seriously. They can be deceptively earnest, but are clearly fond of the schoolboy humour that starts them smirking and leaves them in fits of laughter.

The team have all been members of the Oklahoma Indians' Club for around nine years. They named their vehicle Rez Ride in recognition of their culture (Rez=reservation) and designed it with a keen eye on the anticipated hazards presented by the courses and the other opponents. 'I like to create and work without a plan,' says Paul. 'I like to allow the creation to unfold and adapt to the changing situation.'

The team were aware that RDF would not approve any designs that featured offensive weaponry, and insist that the elements the producers rejected were purely *de*fensive. 'We accepted the rules, but asked if we could include something that could be used to stop another vehicle,' says Edward. 'We had a device that had three bars on it. It dropped from the back of the vehicle. Unfortunately RDF said no to that, even though in our opinion it really was just defensive. We wanted to fit a smoke generator as well, but we didn't tell RDF about that. We didn't do it in the end, but only because we ran out of time.'

The team are a little less forthcoming when I ask them about the water-cannon that they also apparently intended to include. I'm met with a fit of giggles before they deftly change the subject.

'We didn't limit ourselves,' says Leslie, 'and aside from the things RDF said no to there were some things we couldn't do because of the time and budget. We had visions that there would be boulders on the courses, or that we'd be in a maze and would need a radio to help us get out. If we'd had had another two hundred dollars we could have coped with things like that.'

'We had a lot of problems once we started building,' says Paul. 'Our design was unusual, but

'We wanted to fit a smoke generator as well, but we didn't tell RDF about that'

'We didn't get the chance to push it to the limit until something broke'

we chose it for a good reason. We thought that having the extra axle would increase our manoeuvrability. We were trying to get the tightest turning circle we could get, and we thought that if we got stuck then we could lift the wheels up. The third axle is going to be useful because we can drop it down or pick it up. It will do us good on rough terrain.

'We always intended to build a light vehicle,' he continues, 'but once we got the donor car and stripped it down we realised we would have to put some extra weight towards the back end – around 700 pounds, in fact.'

So are there any lingering weight problems? 'Only me!' exclaims Edward, which is a cue for more smirking. Paul regains his composure in time to reassure me that, 'We're fine weight-wise.'

The team's donor vehicle was a four-wheel drive 1976 International Harvester Scout. The extra axle and wheels came from a 1990 Mazda. The two vehicles were merged, along with an awful lot of other parts, with a little help from Edward and Leslie's father. 'Our dad was real supportive,' says Edward. 'He checked the wiring and noticed some things that needed to be changed, and he noticed some other small things. He got the engine running and took care of a lot of the details after that.'

The team had more problems than most in finding the time to construct their vehicle. 'Trying to juggle our personal lives and jobs with all this stuff was real difficult,' says Edward. 'During the first week of the build I had to make a presentation to my senior level class. The week after that was my finals, so I was gone for a whole week. The week after that a close relative, who was also a significant member of our tribe, passed on, so that was big time.'

Paul was also taken away from the build for a week when he participated in some field research for his zoology studies. The team-mates worked on the vehicle when they could, organising shifts and convening at a local restaurant where they discussed their progress over coffee. At the end of the traumatic build they were $300 over budget, but they had confounded RDF's expectations by actually finishing on time. 'They sent an engineer and a film crew out after the second week to see how we were doing,' says Edward. 'They were quite concerned that we hadn't made more progress, and so were we frankly. But we were doing a lot of things for the first time, and although we had only done preliminary work on the vehicle Paul was out getting parts, so it was definitely coming together. If it took us a while that was partly because we were buying a lot of specialist components we'd never bought before, and doing a lot of things to the vehicle we'd never done before.'

'There was no real time to test it at home,' says Paul. 'We didn't get the chance to push it to the limit until something broke. We found the time to drive it around a bit, but that was all really. After that we decided to change the shock absorbers, but that was the only thing. We were amazed at how manoeuvrable it was, actually – even without the working axle. It was surprisingly nimble.'

The team have spent some time wandering around the *FMC* site, trying to work out the nature of the courses by the glimpses they've got of the various structures ('It looks like an amusement park!' remarks a surprised Paul) and checking out the other vehicles.

'I'm worried about The Tartan Tinkerers' vehicle,' says Edward. 'That looks like a big, heavy machine. It's got huge wheels. If that thing hits us then we're in trouble.'

'I'll be OK,' says Leslie, laughing. 'I drive faster than either of you. You drive like old men!'

The Rules

Teams must go through all the gates and not around them. Teams must stay on the course.

My thanks to all the teams and production staff at Full Metal Challenge, but particularly the following especially helpful folk: Greg Bryant, Chantal Burgun, Mike Cotton, Charlotta Hellzen, Andra Heritage, Tiffany Jones, Heidi Lodge, Alex Mahoney, Gemma Ragg, Cathy Rogers, Henry Rollins and Richard Tidsall.

Special thanks to David Breen, Lisa Drury, Claire Kingston, Samantha Kite, Jake Lingwood and Hannah MacDonald, all of whom helped with this particular driving test. I hope I passed.

This book accompanies the television programme Full Metal Challenge made by RDF Media for Channel 4, presented by Henry Rollins and Cathy Rogers.

Supervising Producer – James O'Brien
Project Manager – Greg Bryant
Series Producer – Cathy Rogers

Head of Business Affairs – James McGregor
www.fullmetalchallenge.com

191